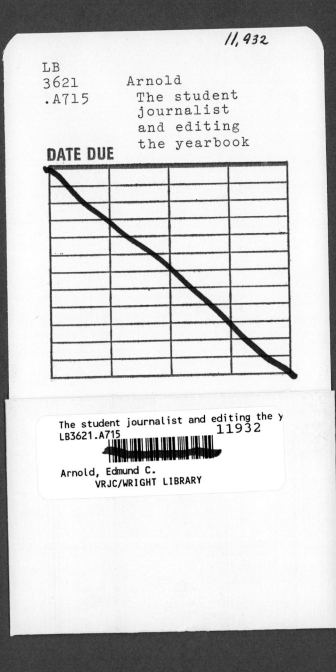

The Student Journalist

and

EDITING
THE
YEAR BOOK

The Student Journalist

and

EDITING
THE
YEAR BOOK

by

Edmund C. Arnold

Chairman Graphic Arts Department
School of Public Communications

Syracuse University

Published by
Richards Rosen
Press Inc.
New York

Standard Book Number: 8239-0279-X
Library of Congress Catalog Card Number: 72-94929
Dewey Decimal Classification: 371.897

Published in 1974 by Richards Rosen Press, Inc.
29 East 21st Street, New York City, N.Y. 10010

Copyright 1974 by Edmund C. Arnold

First Edition
Manufactured in the United States of America

ABOUT THE AUTHOR

EDMUND C. ARNOLD says: "I spend five minutes every day feeling sorry for people who aren't in journalism."

When he makes that observation, he is speaking about every aspect of print journalism. For he has had experience in all of them . . . newspapers, magazines, advertising and as reporter, photographer, editor, advertising salesman and designer and as columnist, author, lecturer and teacher.

He began as editor of a weekly paper at the age of seventeen and even while he served in the Infantry during World War II he was a combat correspondent and editor of service publications, and a Nancy, France, edition staffer for *Stars & Stripes*. Since that time he worked for various newspapers at various jobs, as editor of *Linotype News*, as director of trade relations for the Mergenthaler Linotype Company and, for twenty-one years as editor and co-publisher of *The Frankenmuth News*, a consistent prizewinner in Michigan and nationally. Since 1960 he has been chairman of the graphic arts department at the School of Public Communications at Syracuse University.

But it is as a newspaper designer that he is best known. He designed such outstanding newspapers as *Today* at Cape Kennedy and the *National Observer* and has helped redesign such titans as the *Kansas City Star, Chicago Tribune, Boston Globe, Toronto Star* and *Louisville Courier-Journal* as well as scores of others in the United States and abroad.

He writes a column on the subject for *Editor & Publisher,* and has written over a dozen books, one of which was the first book to win the George A. Polk Memorial Award. One was published in Spanish, another translated into Japanese and the Russians are considering translating another into their language.

He has conducted workshops, seminars and clinics in every state and Canadian province as well as in Central and South American countries. He has led seminars at the American Press Institute and for high school journalism teachers under auspices of the Newspaper Fund.

He has received many professional honors but none he prizes more than the Carl Towley Award and the Pioneer Medal of the National Scholastic Press Association, both for service to scholastic journalism.

Table of Contents

Acknowledgments

Just as most yearbook editors have found out, I have discovered how "plain nice" people can be to an author fighting the long odds of deadlines, typographical errors, human lapses, and the battalions of gremlins who lurk in typewriters. So, just as your yearbook does, this book represents the cooperation of so many people that I can't even begin to count them.

To all of them I extend sincere thanks. I am especially grateful to the scores and scores of editors, staffs, and advisers who have allowed me to use their books as illustrations. I have not identified them in the captions, as in many instances I have made minor changes to demonstrate specific points. And I do not want anyone else to bear the burden of errors I may have thus made. Certainly I have obliterated the identity of those few bad examples that are shown.

Among those whose help must be identified individually are: Marshall Matlock of Arthur Hill High in Saginaw, Michigan; Frank Mohring, Stephen R. Sears, and Bill Celano of William J. Keller Inc.; Jim Thompson of Taylor Publishing Company; Kes Kessler of Inter Collegiate Press, and Frances Webb of Kingsport Covers. And I publicly proclaim what I have told her privately: Without the help of my wife Viola this book would never have come off the typewriter, much less the printing press.

EDMUND C. ARNOLD
Syracuse, New York,

Frozen Time

... The Function of the Yearbook

"Frozen time" is an excellent description of the perfect yearbook. Just as frozen foods capture flavor and nutrition to preserve for the future, then deliver to the consumer the freshness of field or oven, so a good yearbook captures flavor and savor of an academic year. Anytime thereafter, the reader can have this period to enjoy, as bright and exciting as when it was current events instead of history.

To freeze time requires many skills and talents, much hard work, and, most important, loyalty and dedication. That is why yearbook work can be the most rewarding experience of the student.

The yearbook staff learns to work as a team, and no individual achievement can bring laurels quite as green as those won by team effort. The staff makes major—and permanent—contribution to its school and classmates; service is reward in itself. The staff learns discipline, that of working in a chain of command and—the essential of a good life—self-discipline.

The staff's achievement is permanent. Outstanding performances on the dramatic or concert stage, in the classroom or on the athletic field, are short-lived. Ten years from now an important victory in basketball or debate will be forgotten; the yearbook endures, and the quality of your work will be judged over and over.

Such opportunities are a challenge. You can most successfully reap the rich rewards of yearbook work by preparing and mastering your assignments as diligently as professional footballers train or astronauts plot flight plans.

Just what is the job of the yearbook staff?

It is to freeze time. When the reader, a decade or two from now, picks up your book, he should be transported back into the world of his school days. He should feel the excitement of the first day of classes, he should smell the leaves that were burning on the day of the big football game, he should feel the squeak of snow underfoot as he walked up to the door on Junior Prom night, he should hear the recordings to which he studied at night, he should taste the sweetness of success when he mastered a difficult principle in chemistry—and perhaps the salt of defeat when he didn't quite make the Honor Society.

The world that the yearbook mirrors is the school. But the larger world about us also contributes to this year of our lives and must be made part of this record.

Surely, the day man first set foot on the moon was as much a part of the school world and year as the senior play. The death of a great man unites students in a common involvement as deep as that of the night when the team wins the state basketball championship, and we feel, if only momentarily, a unique, memorable brotherhood.

Contents of the Yearbook

To freeze time successfully, the staff needs complete coverage, the highest quality of word and picture, impeccable accuracy, and such a deep knowledge of its world that it can almost instinctively set on paper those connotative trivia that will spur memory and "thaw out" the time between the covers of the book.

As one of the earliest steps in preparing a yearbook, the staff must make an extensive list of the broad areas and specific events to be covered.

The areas do not change from year to year. The most important activity of any school is its academic program. Yet some books ignore this area completely; others pass it off as a trifle.

The classroom should be the primary *beat* for the yearbook staff. It can be as exciting as the sports field and as colorful as the pep rally. The excitement of ideas is intense but it takes a good editor to discern it, to report it, to commit it to good language.

The faculty and administration of a school give it its character and success. This is an important area to cover.

The honorary societies are a reflection of how well the school meets its primary function of education. Cover them well.

Student organizations play a vital part in school life. They are often overplayed in weak yearbooks. But the good editor will give them all the coverage they deserve while recognizing that activities are a secondary part of school life.

Competition makes life interesting, and scholastic competition is no exception. The colorful

Table of Contents

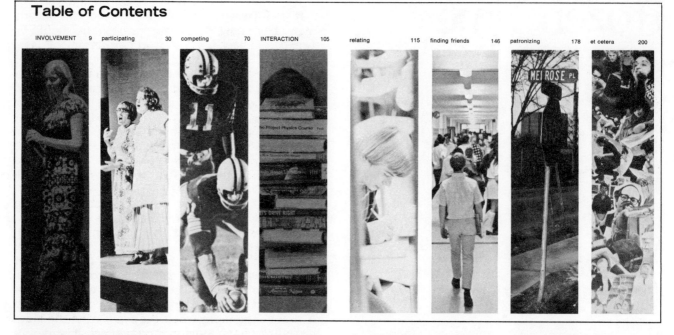

TABLE OF CONTENTS has illustrations to invite reader into book. Instead of traditional sections, there are *Involvement, Participating, Competing, Interaction, Relating, Finding Friends, Patronizing* (not quite the right word!) and *Et Cetera*. It is better to use all nouns or all participles in a series like this rather than to mix them. First and fourth photo panels are duotones in black and yellow.

sports calendar surely deserves adequate coverage in the yearbook but don't overlook the debaters, the forensic teams, and those who compete, as teams or individually, in such activities as Science Fairs, math tournaments, livestock judging, and the many other contests that vary from state to state.

An essential that is often overlooked is commencement. Every yearbook absolutely must have at least one picture and some copy about graduation activities. The editor will usually have to use pictures at least a year old; he must use some picture even if he has to go back a dozen years in the files to find it.

It is important that *all* student activities be covered. Minor, intramural, and girls' sports are often overlooked. Even in major sports, scores are often so buried that they are difficult to find. The season record for each team should be presented in one single tabulation that is conspicuous and easy to find.

Great care must be taken that no club or organization, no matter how little known, is overlooked. Be sure to check your list of organizations against that of the principal or administrator.

Presentation of organizations or individuals should be by "demonstrable priority" to forestall complaints of favoritism.

Arranging individual pictures, or those of clubs,

by alphabetical order is priority that allows little argument. Another way of arranging the order of organizations is by the membership, starting with

Reflections of NHS

TABLE OF CONTENTS is illustrated with unidentified pictures. Traditional sections are used and *Curriculum* gets proper and primary prominence.

Marie Judith Doino

Marianne Donaher . . Chess Club 2; Drama Club 2.

Russel Donahor

Mark Dratch

Christopher Duke

Diane Duncan . . Mixed Chorus 1,2,3.

Deborah Lee Durant

Eddie Dusek . . Concert Band 1,2,3,4 (All-State 1,2,3,4); Concert Orch. 1,2,3,4; Marching Band 1,2,3,4.

Paul James Egan . . Cross Country 2,3,4; Track 1,2,3,4.

Patricia Eisler

Robert Ercole

Conrad John Eschenberg . . Baseball 2; Basketball 2,3; Football 3,4; Track 4.

Gennaro Faiella . . Boy's State 3; M.O.S.T. 1,2,3,4 (Representative 1,2,4; V. Pres. 3); National Honor Society 3,4; School Store 3 (Manager); Track 1,2; Who's Who in American High Schools 4.

Maxine Perl Feld . . Color Guard 3,4 (Co-Capt. 3); Debate Club 2; Home Ec. Club 1,2; Mixed Chorus 1,4; School Store 4; Track Honor Squad 3; Volleyball Honor Squad 2.

Kevin M. Fitzpatrick . . Math Team 4; Soccer 3,4; Track 3.

First Row:
Marie Judith Doino
Marianne Donaher
Second Row:
Russell Donaher
Mark Dratch
Bottom Row:
Christopher Duke
Diane Duncan
Deborah Lee Durant

Class converts
bus into refreshment stand

First Row:
Eddie Dusek
Second Row:
Paul James Egan
Patricia Eisler
Robert Ercole
Third Row:
Conrad John Eschenberg
Gennaro Faiella
Bottom Row:
Maxine Perl Feld
Kevin M. Fitzpatrick

Far Right: Leftover sodas are carried from the senior bus by Patty Gilvey following a home football game.

SENIOR SECTION, always most important in book, carries biographical detail on gray panel. Note how irregular arrangement of portraits adds interest. Quite properly, large picture in lower right is identified, although caption (shown by arrow) is too far away. Gutter margin is too narrow, an all-too-frequent fault in page design.

the largest or smallest. Or the date of its organization can determine the position of a club on a list.

Priority should never be given by any method that cannot be demonstrated. If the staff says the Biology Club is more important than the Spanish Society, the *aficionados* won't agree with that value judgment. But no one can argue that Archaeology comes before Chemistry, by the alphabet. And we can put Sock and Buskin ahead of the Rocket Club if it was formed in 1913 instead of 1970—if all other organizations are also arranged by age. This system is known as that of *demonstrable priorities.*

The staff must lean over backward to avoid even the suspicion that it is playing favorites. Nothing depreciates the value of a yearbook—and takes the luster off the staff's performance—more, or more quickly, than favoritism. If the

book is not truly that of all the school, if a clique or in-group gets preferential treatment, the out-group has every justification for complaint. The usual result is that yearbook sales will drop in future years.

The Senior Section

Time magazine insists that "names make news." Names also make a good yearbook. This is because people are far more interested in people than in things. So people—their faces and their achievements—are an essential part of any yearbook.

The senior class gets greatest personal recognition. Some schools are able to include individual reports on all students, but all will cover the senior class.

Handling information about seniors can develop into an intense headache. The bigger the graduating class, the bigger the pain.

In early yearbooks, each senior's picture was accompanied by his name and a list of his school activities. Often this was expanded by adding his nickname, hobby, favorite food, music, book or

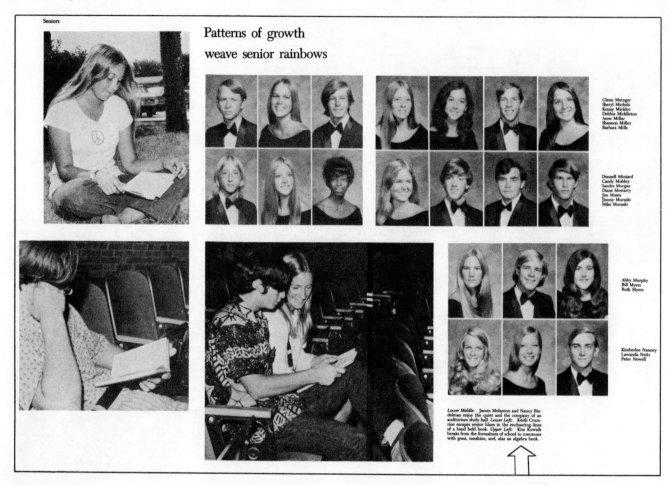

Seniors

Patterns of growth
weave senior rainbows

Glenn Metzger
Sheryl Michels
Kenny Mickler
Debbie Middleton
Anne Millar
Shannon Miller
Barbara Mills

Donnell Miniard
Candy Mobley
Sandra Morgan
Diane Moriarty
Jim Moses
Jimmy Muraski
Mike Muraski

Abby Murphy
Bill Myers
Ruth Myers

Kimberlee Nanney
Lawanda Neitz
Peter Newell

Lower Middle: James Melanson and Nancy Biedelman enjoy the quiet and the company of an auditorium study hall. *Lower Left:* Keith Crumrine escapes senior blues in the enchanting lines of a hand held book. *Upper Left:* Kim Kowalk breaks from the formalness of school to commune with grass, sunshine, and, alas an algebra book.

SENIOR SECTION carries only portraits and larger—and well-identified—candid shots. Senior biographies are presented in separate section. Carrying all photo captions in one block (arrow) puts two of them too far from their pictures. Note uniformity of dress of both girls and boys in portraits.

movie, and other items of similar earthshaking import, as well as a literary quote.

As classes grew larger, it became a major problem to handle all this type and pictures. Complications arose when some students had a list of activities much longer than the rest of those on the page. If each student had the same number of lines of type, it would be relatively simple to make up a page in equal-sized checkerboard units. Uneven copy blocks result in some pages being overcrowded and others shot full of holes.

So the *senior directory* was begun; there, activities were printed separately, and only pictures and identification were run in what became the *senior section.* This solved many problems, but it created even more. It split information that ought to be kept together into two independent—and often widely separated—areas. It created monotonous picture pages, since each senior picture must be identical in size and treatment to all others. It jammed lots of type into pages often unrelieved by art.

Just as a picture enlivens large areas of type, so a block of type can relieve a pageful of pictures. Photography—especially a group of portraits—can get as monotonous as a page of solid type; we can lose our appetite for ice cream as fast as for bread.

Therefore, the ideal book will present all vital statistics, photographic and verbal, about seniors in one section. It will make more work for the staff, true. But no one ever said that a good yearbook is an easy job.

In some parts of the country, especially the East, the yearbook is traditionally "the seniors' book." Underclassmen rarely buy a copy. This is unfortunate. Surely a person's sophomore year is as important as his senior year. A good yearbook will be one that belongs to every student, not just to the graduating class.

As the book records individual activities, it will most certainly not overlook those of underclassmen.

The last area is the greater world around the school. Coverage will depend on specific events.

Senior Biography

ABNEY, ADA LORRAINE. Moss Point, Mississippi. Business Administration and Marketing. Transfer student from Jackson County Junior College. A member of Afro American Cultural Society.
ABRAHAM, WILLIAM BRYON. Port Gibson, Mississippi.
ACREY, DONALD OLIVER, JR. Amarillo, Texas.
ADAMS, DANNY LEE. Smithdale, Mississippi. Finance.
ADAMS, GERALD JOE. Gautier, Mississippi.
ADAMS, RONALD HARVEY. Pensacola, Florida.
ADERHOLDT, MARGARET B. Clarksdale, Mississippi.
AGALL, BILL G. Hattiesburg, Mississippi.
AIKENS, WALTER BARCLAY. Mobile, Alabama.
AINSWORTH, JOHN HAROLD. Laurel, Mississippi.
AINSWORTH, JULIA ANN. Magee, Mississippi.
AINSWORTH, SARAH REBECCA. Laurel, Mississippi. Elementary Education. Dean's List.
AITCHESON, FRANK L., III. Orlando, Florida. Political Science. Sigma Alpha Epsilon. President; Secretary of Sigma Alpha Epsilon Fraternity; Sigma Alpha Epsilon pledge class, Vice President; Sigma Alpha Epsilon Province Convention Delegate and Inter Fraternity Council Representative.
ALBRITTON, CHARLOTTE M. Picayune, Mississippi.
ALBRYCHT, JOHN J. Ocean Springs, Mississippi. Computer Science. Association of Computing Machinery, Dean's List.
ALEXANDER, DAVID HAROLD. Little Rock, Mississippi.
ALEXANDER, NITA LORRAINE. Jackson, Mississippi. Speech Therapy. Sigma Alpha Eta Fraternity (Speech & Hearing) Treasurer; Baptist Student Union Choir (B.S.U.); B.S.U. Devotional Chairman; Bolton Dorm Treasurer.
ALFONSO, TOMMYE CARLENE. Gulfport, Mississippi.
ALFORD, JEWEL WAYNE. Poplarville, Mississippi. Biology, G.D.I.
ALFORD, RANDAL PRISOCK. Jackson, Mississippi.
ALFORD, VERNA D. Columbia, Mississippi. Executive Secretarial Studies. The Afro-American Cultural Society, Secretary, The U.A.C.
ALLEN, DEANE. Leland, Mississippi.
ALLEN, PRENTISS DANIEL. Magnolia, Mississippi. General Business.
ALLEN, RICHARD DOUGLAS. Magnolia, Mississippi. Business Administration. Kappa Sigma. Pi Sigma Epsilon (Marketing), Master Mason; Inter Fraternity

Council (2 Years).
ALLEN, ROBERT SPENCER. Gulfport, Mississippi.
ALLEN, SCOTT RAY. Neshoba, Mississippi.
ALLISON, THOMAS IRVIN. Union, Mississippi.
ALLMON, CAROLYN SUE. Seminary, Mississippi. Business Education. Pi Omega Pi, Second Vice President; Student Education Association; National Business Education Association; Dean's List.
ANDERSON, AUDREY, ELLEN. Gulfport, Mississippi. Clothing Merchandising. Dean's List.
ANDERSON, CHRISTINA LOU. Seminary, Mississippi. Special Education. President's List; Who's Who Among Students in American Colleges and Universities; Wesley Foundation Secretary; Council for Exceptional Children Secretary; Kappa Delta Pi Secretary, Senior Year Traineeship in Special Education; Student Education Association.
ANDERSON, JAMES MICHAEL. Gulfport, Mississippi.
ANDERSON, TIMOTHY NORWOOD. Jackson Mississippi.
ANDERSON, TIMOTHY SIMS. Gulfport, Mississippi.
ANDING, BRENDA GAIL. Brookhaven, Mississippi.
ANDREWS, BEKGY KAY. Vicksburg, Mississippi.
ANDREWS, BERTHA. Hattiesburg, Mississippi.
ANGE, SANFRA LYNN. Edenton, North Carolina. General Business. Delta Delta Delta. Dixie Darling Captain and Dixie Darlin (3 years); Pom Pom Girl (3 years), Circle Favorite, ROTC Sponsor, Song Chairman of Delta Delta Delta, Phi Tau Chi Religious Honorary Society, Assistant Social Chairman of Delta Delta Delta, Miss Dau District of North Carolina.
ANTULLIS, CHARLES P., JR. Burlington, Mass.
ARD, CENCILIA RUTH. Pascagoula, Mississippi. History.

leges and Universities, Member of Dixie Darlings, Representative of Dixie Darling Council, Vice-president of Phi Delta Rho, Treasurer of Druids, Member of Alpha Lambda Delta, Member of Alpha Sigma Alpha, Philanthropic Chairman of Alpha Sigma Alpha; Devotional Chairman of Alpha Sigma Alpha Pledge Class, Member of Pi Tau Chi, Freshman Orientation Committee, Member of Student Christian Federation (SCF), Member of SCF Executive Board, SCF Secretary, Member of Committee of 100, Member of Committee 50, Member of Student Religious Federation (SRF), Member of SRF Executive Board, Constitution Chairman of SCF, Dean's List Scholar, Received General merit Scholarship, President of Dormitory, Member of Association of Women Students, Member of Beta Beta Beta—Biology List.
ASKIN, LOUIS JOSEPH, JR. Biloxi, Mississippi.
ATKINSON, JOYE FLORENCE. Biloxi, Mississippi. Institution Management - Dietetics. Home Economics Club—Sophomore, Junior year. Kappa Omicron Phi—Junior, Senior member. Vice President Kappa Omicron Phi—Sophomore, Junior year. Dean's List.
ATKINSON, WALTER CARLOS. Panama City, Florida.
AUSTIN, LARRY LIDELL. Hattiesburg, Mississippi.
AUTREY, JERRY BROOK. Batesville, Mississippi. Personnel Management. Kappa Alpha. Kappa Alpha House Manager, Recording Secretary (NO. 3) Inter Fraternity Council.
AYCOCK, CARL JACKSON.

Killing time. Waiting for something, someone. Slow motion while the world runs away. Wondering when "the" events will occur—living for them—surviving between them.

BARFIELD, THOMAS FOSTER. Selma, Alabama.
BARKLEY, TIMOTHY BRYON. Waveland, Mississippi.
BARNES, CYNTHIA LAFAYE. Eight Mile, Alabama.
BARNES, JANIS DEAN. Hattiesburg, Mississippi.
BARNETT, LINDA JANELL. Music Education. Tau Beta Sigma—Social Chairman, Mu Phi Epsilon, Music Educators National Conference. Pride of Mississippi Marching Band. USM Concert Band.
BARNETT, GEORGE BARRY. Ellisville, Mississippi.
BARNETT, MORRIS GLENN, JR. Hattiesburg, Mississippi. Mathematics.
BARNHILL, MEREDITH RICHMON. Hattiesburg, Mississippi.
BARR, CHRISTOPHER CARWIN Raymond, Mississippi.
BARRETT, JERRY EDWIN. Carson, Mississippi.
BARRETT, JUDITY CROLYN. Gulfport, Mississippi.
BARRY, ELEANOR MAE. Jackson, Mississippi. Personnel Management, Business Administration. Recording Secretary of Society for Advancement of Management.
BARTON, CAROL HUMPHREY. Ebenezer, Mississippi.
BASHAM, GLENN EMORY. Ellisville, Mississippi.
BASS, JAMES MARVIN. Enterprise, Mississippi.
BASS, PHILLIP B. Bassfield, Mississippi. Marine Biology. Dean's List, Progressive Students Association.
BATEMAN, LARRY D. Meridian, Mississippi. Personnel Management.
BATEMAN, MARTIN KARR.

352

SENIOR BIOGRAPHIES are carried alphabetically in second-last section of this book. Candid shot and caption in larger type relieve large mass of 6-point bios.

During some years, the outside world is well removed from the school world. In other years, momentous events, local, national, or international, have touched the students so deeply that the events have become an integral part of our smaller scholastic world. The effect they had on the student will, naturally, determine how extensive the coverage.

Each of these beats will have individual events that must be recorded. Here, a search of past yearbooks, files of the school and local newspapers, and the official calendar kept by the principal will give a detailed list.

The first day of school is a memorable one; it must be reported. Organization of clubs, class elections, sports events, dramatic and musical presentations, assemblies and honors convocations, election campaigns—details vary among schools but the list is a long one and doesn't vary too much from year to year.

Of course, the staff must also be alert to the unexpected.

If a fire breaks out in the cafeteria, a prominent person visits your campus or town, or an unexpected snowstorm disrupts class schedules, the yearbook staff must be prepared to record these events in words and pictures.

But the meat of any yearbook will be perennial events. So the first job of coverage is to make a detailed list and assign specifics to reporters. Intense perusal of past yearbooks, your own and those of other schools, and files of local and student newspapers are the major sources. Each editor should keep a complete diary of school events during his tenure to pass on to his successor, for whom they will become part of a basic list.

Assignments should be made early, and follow-up should be close and constant.

Dedication

A recurring problem is that of dedications.

The tradition of dedicating a book to an individual dates back to Gutenberg. At first such dedications thanked a patron for financial subsidy of author or work. Then dedications became expressions of affection, usually to a relative or close

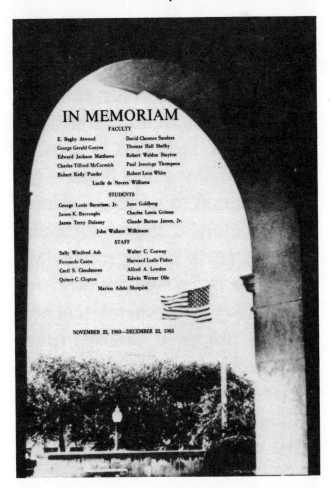

IN MEMORIAM PAGE is handled simply and with great dignity. Half-staff flag is appropriate sign of mourning. Care must be taken that religious symbols of one religion are not used to honor dead of another faith.

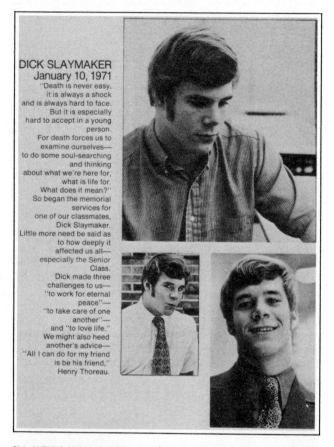

DICK SLAYMAKER
January 10, 1971
"Death is never easy, it is always a shock and is always hard to face. But it is especially hard to accept in a young person.
For death forces us to examine ourselves—to do some soul-searching and thinking about what we're here for, what is life for. What does it mean?"
So began the memorial services for one of our classmates, Dick Slaymaker. Little more need be said as to how deeply it affected us all—especially the Senior Class.
Dick made three challenges to us—"to work for eternal peace"—"to take care of one another"—and "to love life."
We might also heed another's advice—"All I can do for my friend is be his friend,"
Henry Thoreau.

IN MEMORIAM PAGE avoids even that phrase as it shows candids of deceased classmate. Copy is well written, sincere without being maudlin.

friend. Yearbook dedications most often single out a faculty member for admiration and respect.

Such a dedication is a commendable gesture. Often teachers well deserve such recognition. But the dedication should be a genuine and spontaneous one. And if the staff doesn't feel strongly impelled to dedicate its book, there is no law that says it has to.

A dedication resembles in many ways the rarer *In Memoriam*. Although high school students are, as a group, in the prime of health, deaths do occur within the student body, as among the faculty, and should be recorded in a yearbook.

Often a book is dedicated to the dead person. This, incidentally, is the only time dedication should be made to a student. The memorial page may be in addition to the customary dedication.

In both instances these are sentimental pages. The writer must avoid maudlin sentimentality. A too-sugary treatment will repel the reader and embarrass the subject or his family. Americans, by training, are not very demonstrative about things that arouse strong feelings. We get exuberant over a football team but are reticent about people we care for deeply. But we understand each other's understatement. So these memorial and

dedication pages should be written simply, without embellishment. If the writer feels deeply about his subject, that genuine emotion will shine through his words and be all the stronger because of his restraint.

Progression

Once the contents of the yearbook have been determined, the question is: In what order should they be presented? This is the *progression* of the book.

Progression is an important factor in a successful book. It contributes to the reader's pleasure and enhances communication.

Contents can be arranged in many ways, each of which may be just as good as any other. Conventionally, a book opens with a section devoted to faculty and administration. Usually ACTIVITIES are next presented, then sports, classes, and, finally, graduating seniors. There is nothing wrong with such progression. But it should be emphasized that there is nothing sacred about it, either.

A good yearbook may be compared to a musical composition. There are an infinite number of ways in which the notes on the scale can be arranged to create a pleasant melody. But all music is like all other; it has a beginning and an end and a smooth, pleasant transition between. So the yearbook must begin and end with a solid chord while the material in between is presented in the most pleasing way.

Because the primary function of a school is academic, it is appropriate to begin the book with that topic. Faculty and administration are important; they are the continuing influence that makes a school an enduring institution rather than one that changes character and direction every four years. But these topics need not be at the beginning of the book in order to carry importance.

The senior picture gallery often runs at the end of the book because their graduation is the end and climax of the school year.

An interesting progression is to group subjects by the calendar. Events that happened in September open the book; those of springtime are at the end. Football is in the fall section and basketball in winter, rather than having them grouped together under SPORTS.

An advantage of this system is that it enables the staff to meet deadlines with greater ease. Sections can be completed and sent to the printer on a more regular schedule. In normal progression, the sports editor cannot wind up his section until spring sports are completed. Under the seasonal arrangement, the calendar marks the end of each section.

A new technique that has been used by successful books is to open with an illustrated essay. This records the history of the entire four school years of the graduates. It can be a highly evocative as well as informative section. It sets the tone for the entire book and gives a continuity and a unity that is necessary for a superlative yearbook.

A continuing—and probably major—problem of the editor is to create such *unity*. Too many yearbooks are fragmented, There is little if any connection between the various sections. Each section editor may adopt his own style of writing and layout. The result is several small booklets that just happen to be bound into one cover.

But the yearbook must be a single book. While each section may be reasonably self-contained, there must be a harmonious interrelationship with all others.

VISUALIZING THEME is done in simple line drawings, well suited to "The Year in Profile." Note how basic figures are modified. Each one becomes identifier of one section of book.

The Theme

The most useful thread to tie various sections together is the yearbook *theme*. This is a device—visual, verbal, and psychological—that defines the point of view or the common reference to which all parts of the yearbook are directed.

Every once in a while an editor decides to put out a book without a theme. He feels this is a corny idea; if anything has been used for sixty years it must be shopworn. Unfortunately, there are some elements of truth in his condemnation. Too often themes are unimaginative, overblown clichés. Or they are used poorly, never quite achieving their primary function. But a well-chosen, well-handled theme can be invaluable to the editor; it can help make a brighter, more appealing book.

The editor really can't put out a book without a theme. He may not use an obvious one, but the unifying idea—the theme—that permeates any yearbook is: This is the way life was in our school. Without this theme, there would be no yearbook. The more obvious theme is but a device to allow pleasant presentation of the materials created by the basic theme.

Choosing the theme is the first creative work of the staff. This should be done in the spring the year before publication, since almost every job of the editor and staff will be dependent on the theme.

The staff should explore all potentials, disadvantages, and ramifications of the theme before committing itself. They will study the files of previous yearbooks, not only in their own school but all others in the city or area.

No editor would want to present to the senior class a theme that had been used during its sophomore year. Nor would you want your theme this year to be the same as your crosstown rivals used last year.

In theory, a theme ought to be reusable every five years. Actually the same theme could be used on consecutive years as imaginative handling would remove all repetition. But the typical staff prefers a theme as new as possible so its creativity will not be clouded by even unconscious copycatting.

The theme must be appropriate and logical. A New Mexico high school would find a theme on Navajo Indians colorful and exciting; but in upper New York State, the staff would choose the Iroquois. A Yankee Clipper sailing ship theme would be ideal for a Cape Cod school but a little ridiculous for one in Salt Lake City.

But the theme need not be restrictive. An editor may choose American Indians as his theme; then he could include the exotic Navajos and the fierce Blackfeet as well as those native to his area. Or a Kansas editor could choose transportation **as his**

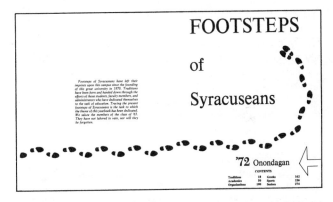

THEME OF BOOK is given greater prominence than its name (arrow) in this two-page title page. The footstep motif . . .

. . . is carried throughout book, not only on divider pages. More unity could be achieved by using same typeface on all introductory pages.

"Tis what the body together   can do that carries the victory far."

ATHLETICS

What are sports at Syracuse? More than a nationally acclaimed football team, a rising lacrosse team, a good track team and a promising basketball team. Sports comprise the Greek idea of a sound body governed by a well-conditioned mind. Whether the student is a participating athlete or a spirited observer he makes up the "body together" which "carries the victory far." . . . Athletics at Syracuse are more than a pastime— they play an important part in the development of each student.

"DEVELOPING THEME" uses seal of university. One element of the seal is printed in orange, school color, rest in black, for each section of book. For *Athletics*—shown here—university name is in color. For *Academics,* the word "University" is colored. *Traditions* has lower arc, "Founded A.D. 1870"; *Seniors* has the motto, "Knowledge crowns those who seek her." Wreath is for *Honors,* of course, and for closing, farewell section, whole seal is in color.

theme; then sailing ships would be as logical as covered wagons and railroads.

A good theme should be an enduring one. If we are writing this book for an audience twenty years in the future, the theme must be as meaningful then as it is today.

Do not build a theme on a person of momentary popularity. The hero of a television show, a million-record singer, the performer of some extraordinary (but insignificant) feat will be forgotten long before the pages of our book get dog-eared. Do not peg your book on an event of transient interest.

Newspapers can furnish ideas for good themes. The first landing on the moon made an excellent theme; a September heat wave is by its nature of short life and interest. On the other hand, we can expand that topic to weather in general and that would make an excellent theme, especially in areas that have four distinct seasons. Even though we are not as dependent on meteorology as a farmer or sailor, all of us are affected by the weather and have a great interest in it. The more

universal the involvement of your readers in a theme, the greater its appeal and effectiveness.

A good theme must be universal—broad, rather than specific, in scope. Let us assume that the theme is *A Day at Ourtown High.* We start by showing a student rolling out of bed, eating breakfast, dashing for the school bus, in classes and labs—the routine so typical that it is in itself universal. But if we show the same student over and over, not only may monotony set in, it is difficult for even the most typical member of the student body to represent the whole group. Yet if we use a different student for each picture, we destroy the unity that a theme must give.

The solution?

Instead of showing the student, let's picture only his (or her or their) feet. By shooting from a low angle, we can show proper backgrounds. We can show seasonal or time changes by varying the shoes—bedroom slippers, loafers, overshoes, sneakers, athletic shoes, casuals, and dressups. Now every reader can almost literally put himself in the model's shoes. Now our model is no longer Bill Jones; he's Everyman.

We might show hands at various scholastic jobs. Again the member is more universal than the whole body.

Or we might take an inanimate but universal object. We can show a pencil on a pile of books alongside a breakfast plate. The same pencil can be doing calculus or doodling or diagraming a football play. It can be making marginal notes on a theater program or an athletic score card. Finally, it can be making an entry in a diary or autographing a yearbook.

The actual books used during one high school career can be used for a dramatically striking *expanding theme,* a term soon to be discussed. Start with the student handbook that many schools provide, or with the books used in freshman year. Keep adding advanced books, texts, workbooks, notebooks, and bluebooks until the final impressive pile is topped with a mortarboard or diploma. By highlighting the title on one or a few books, the appropriate sections of the yearbook can be introduced.

Another universal element of unusual pictorial flexibility are the bulletin boards that abound in any school. The casual observer thinks all bulletin boards are alike. Yet, by content if not by form, each has a flavorful individuality. The board in the boys' gym is markedly different from that in the home ec room, for instance.

It is easy to tack up an extra piece of paper or cardboard to carry the name of the book section or a suitable quotation. Many bulletins also accommodate three-dimensional objects that can easily be changed to reenforce the theme.

Architecture makes interesting pictorial variations to carry out a theme. If yours is an older school, you will probably be surprised at the wide variety of doors and windows. If yours is a sterile modern building, it would not be amiss to wander through town and find architectural details of variety, as well as of interest and symbolism. Those on the courthouse or church can stand for tradition, on a ticket booth for activities, on a store for advertising, and so on.

Paintings in your school halls or local museum, books in the school or public library, front pages of newspapers, trophies, medals, and keys; record jackets or sheet music; posters that adorn all schools or those from local theaters—any of these, and countless others, make intriguing themes.

A good theme must have visual as well as verbal appeal. Themes are developed by words, photographs, and hand art. Unless your theme can be communicated through pictures as well as words, it will fail.

If the theme is one that can be developed in stages, an *expanding theme,* it adds great appeal. The editor turns static pages into almost moving pictures. Indeed, the technique is much like that used by Hollywood for its opening titles and credits.

An example would be the use of local maps as a theme. The first visual presentation would show the confluence of a couple of streams and the trading post that was the nucleus of your city. This could be used for the TRADITIONS section of your book. In the second visual, the rivers and post would be shown in gray and, in black, would be added several of the early log cabins to introduce the section on PEOPLE. In the third development, the first school could be indicated in black, all the previous elements in gray; this could be ACADEMICS.

Thus the visual device is expanded. Each new element is shown in black; the previous ones are in gray. Ultimately the whole map would be completed.

Many devices can be used in this visual development. Blueprints used for a new school are ideal for this purpose. The seal or coat-of-arms of your school, city or state can be built up this way, each element symbolizing one section of your book.

The good theme must always be subordinate to the content of the book. If the theme is too obtrusive, too cute, or too stretched, it will detract from the book proper and will irritate the reader rather than please him.

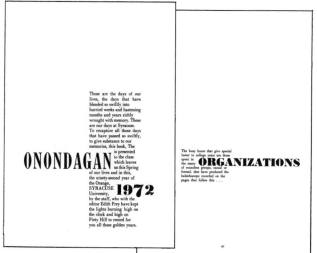

TYPOGRAPHIC REPETITION gives unity to this book. Title page is at left; typical section page has display type in same position. Fragment of divider page (right) shows how emphasized word reads right into copy.

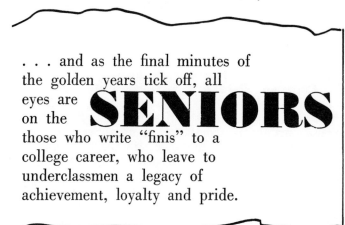

"Cute" or "stretched" themes are illogical or inappropriate. When the editor must bend logic and extend deductions to force the theme into the book, the result cannot be happy.

A growingly popular theme device—even though it may not be called that by the editor—is to use the lyrics of a popular song as running heads, divider-page copy, or even captions in the forematter of a yearbook. This is an excellent technique because of the highly evocative nature of music and also because the words—grown familiar to the reader by great repetition and written by skilled professionals—often express the moods of school years most accurately.

Unfortunately, this technique may expose the staff to embarrassment and punishment!

All published songs are copyrighted; no one may reprint them without specific permission of the copyright holder.

If the copyright is violated, the offender can be sued for damages he has sustained, and additional —and large—amounts of money may be demanded as punishment. And, of course, there is the humiliation of being publicly identified as a lawbreaker.

Unfortunately, the copyright law is broken every day in most schools; every time someone Xeroxes a page of a copyrighted book, he is breaking the law and leaving himself open to a lawsuit. The common alibi that "I am doing this for educational purposes" is no valid excuse. Fortunately most authors and publishers are forgiving and do not sue the violators.

But because the pirating of music has been so widespread, and financial loss to the legitimate publishers has been so great, they have been forced to active policing of their copyrights. It is inevitable that one of these days they will make an example of some miscreant and thus put the fear of the law into the heart of everyone else. It would be somewhat less than delightful if your staff were to become that public example.

If you want to use copyrighted material, be sure to ask permission from the publisher. In most cases it will be granted, graciously and promptly. If it is not, seek other material to quote.

It is ironic that as more and more staffs are violating the copyright laws, more and more staffs are seeking the protection of the very same laws. It has become fashionable to copyright a yearbook. This may gratify the egos of the staff, but it is an unnecessary and pretentious exercise.

Copyright laws are designed to protect the property rights of the creators of verbal, visual, or musical forms. The royalties are the only recompense an author, composer, or artist receives for his work. To copy that work in part or whole, without paying royalties is truly piracy. It is stealing the fruit of a person's labors (and you know how much labor goes into the making of a book!)

TYPOGRAPHIC MOTIF, strong in weight and contemporary in feeling, ties together sections of this book. But all-black pages, though striking in appearance, can pose difficulties to pressmen, and such usage cannot be highly recommended.

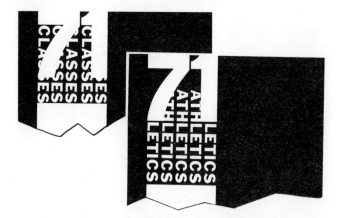

exactly as if a thug stole the salary of a working person or if someone refused to pay a doctor, lawyer, or carpenter for services they have rendered.

But there is no commercial gain to be obtained by copying all or part of a high school or college yearbook. Who would want to copy your yearbook, for instance? How could anyone make any money from doing that? And if someone did, who would be damaged thereby? No one.

So there is no need to copyright a yearbook, and to do so seems a grandiose affectation.

How does the staff select a theme?

First, look at yearbooks in your library. Ideas generate ideas. You don't want to copy themes, but as you look at the work of your predecessors, you will be stimulated to ideas of your own.

Books of quotations are an excellent source. They immediately provide the articulation of the theme.

History books of all kinds can give inspiration. However, remember the formula: $I \sim d$. I(interest) is inversely proportionate to d(distance): the closer something comes to the reader, the more interested he is. So the history of your country would have more inherent appeal than that of the Crusades.

Magazines and newspapers can give you ideas.

The staff of a California school found its inspiration in an exchange student from Uruguay. Their book used the Latin American theme with all the colorful accoutrements of our friends south of the Rio Grande. In the opening section, copy was carried in Spanish and English.

Many themes can be carried out on two levels of thought. Shakespeare gave us "All the world's a stage." If this were our theme, on the literal level we would show the picturesque world of backstage

HAND ART makes strong divider pages, especially as contrast to heavy use of photography, typical of today's books. Any art, however, should be used only if its quality is high.

with all the distinctive paraphernalia of theatricals. Or we could use Shakespeare's analogy of the development of the individual from infancy to maturity. Or we could go one step further; we could use scenes or quotations from famous dramas to introduce sections of the book.

A good theme must be in good taste, simple, logical, appropriate, and amenable to visualization.

The theme begins on the cover of the book, and the very first page of the book proper should give the reader a clear and concise picture of the theme and a suggestion on how it will be developed.

Divider pages, which introduce each new section, are major tools for the development of the theme. Visual, verbal, or mnemonic devices pertaining to the theme may be used on any page. If there are no dividers, because of the *running copy* of the book, the theme must be developed in regular text pages, of course.

Anatomy of the Book

The tradition of the book is long and honorable; the first product, over 400 years ago, of the printing press and movable type was a book. Because the yearbook is primarily a book, it is appropriate that it share some characteristics with all books.

The editor should examine the anatomy of a good book; he will find it interesting. Notice that after the end papers comes a *half title*, a page with only the name of the book on it; two pages later is the full *title page*. Only in recent years has

TITLE PAGES properly give name of school, city, and state. Both "Towers" are in black-and-white. "Blueprint" uses full process color; "Bronze Book" has brilliant blue and green in spot color.

this been sometimes expanded to a *spread,* two facing pages. After a page containing *copyright notices* and Library of Congress *indicia* may come a dedication, certain *forematter*—preface, foreword, index, and so on, all before the text of the book starts.

Yearbook editors do not have pages to leave blank. So the book conventionally begins on the first text page, where the half title used to go. This may be a title page or it may introduce a two-page title spread. There is absolutely nothing mandatory about this progression. If it pleases the reader, any progression is good.

Traditionally, the title page of a book sets its theme, be it a novel or a scientific reference work. The same applies even more so to the yearbook. The title page or spread gives the name of the book, date of publication, and the name and place of the school. Sometimes the *masthead* (carrying the names of all staffers) appears on this page; sometimes only the editor in chief and business manager are listed here. Sometimes all the staff is named elsewhere.

In addition to this information, some visual presentation of the theme will be a major decorative element on the title page.

A new device is to start the book with introductory matter, perhaps the illustrated essay, and make the title page a logical development within this introduction. Sometimes the title page will not appear until as late as page 20 or so.

This is, obviously, an adaption of the Hollywood technique in which the movie begins with the story, and credits are not shown until the audience has been captured by the action.

To capture the audience's attention immediately should be the aim of the staff. Ideally, you should turn the *looker* into a *reader* as soon as possible, so it is logical to start out with copy that has great impact.

The staff should be warned that handling the title page in this delayed fashion may lose it points in yearbook contests. Often it takes a long time for new techniques to be incorporated in official scoresheets. This is annoying and disappointing to the staff, of course. But you can console yourself with the truth that acceptance by your student body is a far greener laurel wreath than an All-American rating.

The art editor should seek pleasant variety in developing the theme visually. If yours is a device that can be developed in stages, there can be enough variety in the growth to avoid monotony. If yours is not an expanding theme, then seek maximum variety in the subject matter. A large school that chose the theme *Key to Knowledge,* used woodblocks as decorations. Variety came from the variety of keys used for illustrations. They ranged from the small ones used for suitcases to those about two feet long that locked the doors of ancient castles.

If photography is used for the theme subject, there must be enough continuity in pose, subject, angle, or lighting to let the reader know immediately that this is a theme picture and not a random snapshot.

Words—in text or headlines—must explore and expand on the theme. For this the editor must demand the ultimate in literary excellence. This copy will most usually be brief. Brevity is a virtue as far as the reader is concerned; but to the writer it imposes a heavy burden. It is much more difficult to write fifty eloquent words than to express

HALF-TITLE PAGE is often omitted in contemporary books. Here that page (left) shows only longhorn symbol of Texas school. Typical section page (right) repeats symbol as unifying visual theme. Panel at bottom is bright blue.

the same thought in a thousand words. *Rewriting* is the secret to good theme copy, and its brevity makes rewriting less of a mechanical chore. The editor must remind his staff that in the standard television contract, the playwright is committed to do two complete rewrites. Many more rewrites are normal. If these skilled and experienced professionals must rewrite this extensively, surely the student author shouldn't feel insulted when the editor insists on reworking of copy.

Running headlines (discussed in detail in Chapter III) are useful in developing the theme.

Rarely do students choose a humorous theme. They seem to feel that humor detracts from dignity or quality. Abraham Lincoln's wit rebuts that; in a later day, President Kennedy lost no authority because of the light touch with which he leavened many a situation.

Humor can be used effectively if it is done in good taste. It should never be cruel, even unconsciously so. It is saddening that in the place where humor frequently appears in yearbooks—in quotations describing seniors—it should be misused. Many a young person has been wounded by humor that misfired. It is ironic that the high school student, who is so sensitive to opinions of his peers, should be so careless when he is the giver instead of the receiver of wise- (or not-so-wise) cracks.

When humor is used, it should be subjected to the most critical appraisal by the editor and staff. If there is the slightest possibility that someone might be hurt, throw it out! If there must be errors, let them be on the side of charity.

In-jokes have absolutely no place in any student publication. The yearbook, especially, should avoid those oblique references that will send a half-dozen students into paroxysms of laughter—while the other hundreds of the student body are merely puzzled. Such private humor never wears

well, either. Even the tiny minority that may see something funny in an obscure anecdote today will find it incredibly stupid in a month or two.

Always, the staff must remember that the theme is definitely subordinate to the real content of the book. Undue emphasis on the theme can be annoying or boring. Often such prominence indicates that the theme was poorly chosen, that it must be inflated artificially. The good theme is unobtrusive; that's the way it should be.

Because a yearbook is produced in small units, it demands unusual care and skill to make sure that all the pieces interlock into an attractive and harmonious whole.

As soon as the theme is selected, the whole staff should be told about it. The choice, in most schools, is the prerogative of the editor in chief. In some instances the senior editors choose it collectively. In all cases, the advice of the adviser should be sought.

The editor should explain why the theme was selected and tell how he envisions it will be used throughout the book. Then each section editor should ponder, long and hard, on how the theme can be used in his section. In staff meetings, each editor should tell his plans so that adjustments can be made if necessary.

The editors in charge of photography and hand art should express the theme visually with rough drawings. In staff meetings the necessary harmonizing of words and pictures should be discussed in considerable detail.

All such planning should be done in the spring and summer. By the time the staff returns to school, it should be ready to plunge right into production.

Now the editor's most important job begins. He—personally and alone—must give the unity that will transform many small elements into a single, good book.

As soon as copy is written and layouts made, the editor should inspect them with meticulous care. He should note, not only that these elements meet standards in themselves, but also that they will blend smoothly into sections before and after.

Unfortunately, the book is not produced in consecutive order. Therefore the editor must read the carbons of copy and look at the duplicate dummies of earlier materials as he reads the current production. Even if this creates extra work or becomes boring, the editor must discipline himself to this process in order to maintain the necessary total harmony.

An important factor in such harmony is the ending of the book. The editor should notice how a musical composition closes. The composer recapitulates the whole number and makes of the ending a satisfying climax. The yearbook also should come to a definite end. It should not peter out in insipid disorganization.

A few brave editors will keep the last several pages for a strong pictorial layout and expressive copy. The principal's parting message seems a logical way to close a book. Or the class prophecy or poem (if they are good—too often they are not) may be the finale.

Advertising Placement

Such treatment means that advertising must be moved from its customary place at the very back of the book to some earlier place. This is another innovation to which contest judges react violently; but there is no justification for this punitive attitude.

There is nothing sinful about advertising that it must be sealed off lest it contaminate editorial content. Just as soon as a staff sells advertising, it recognizes the legitimate worth of ads and it publicly proclaims that its book is an advertising medium. Advertising runs cheek by jowl with editorial copy in the finest magazines in America; there is absolutely no logical reason why ads cannot run anywhere in a yearbook. If advertising is properly created by the yearbook staff, it will be as interesting and appealing to the reader as editorial matter.

ADVERTISING is integral part of this book. Page with four ads (left) is handled exactly like page of editorial content at right. "Selling" copy in ads is presented in captions.

A common component of many yearbooks is the *index*. Its value is dubious, however, and the staff should thoroughly consider its value before committing themselves to its use.

Indexes take valuable space; they require arduous, plodding labor; they constantly pose the problems of classification—under what heading should an item be indexed? And all the while, grave doubt of its necessity gnaws at us. In fact, indexes are probably used far more often because staffs fear their absence will penalize them in a contest rather than because of firm conviction of their usefulness.

A book of many hundreds of pages, as one of a large university, may conceivably require an index, even though that premise can be vigorously debated. Surely, a smaller book does not. In fact, an index may reduce readership; the person who is searching for a face or name will be exposed to many more pages than he who goes to an index—and then on to only one or two pages.

A *table of contents* is another unnecessary space-waster. If it can be worked into a theme page, the table is not utterly wasted. But it is a rare reader who will use it to single out only one section for perusal.

Staffs ought to give serious thought to some other common practices that seem to have outgrown their usefulness—if they ever had any. If, after consideration, the staff decides to retain such

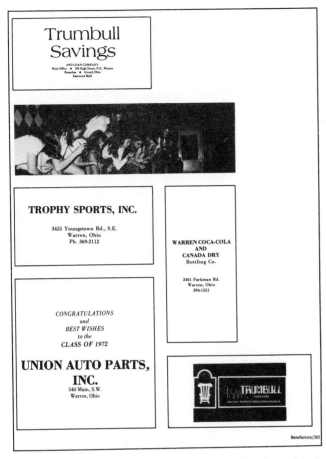

ADVERTISING PLACEMENT is handled in same informal balance as are editorial pages. This is pleasant change from stiff rectangles of typical yearbook advertising pages.

cult to be appropriate; much less witty.

Even more dangerous are the selection of *The Boy Most Likely to Succeed* and similar projections of the future. Too often these are dismal failures in prognostication. Twenty years from now, every inaccurate prophecy is a sore spot. Ask your parents how often *The Boy Most* found that a winning smile and the ability to softsoap student body and faculty failed to deceive the cold, cold world. And how often the quiet, overlooked fellow in the back row wound up owning half a city. The

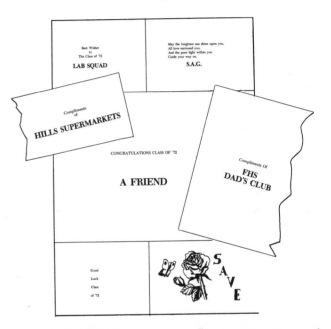

POOR ADVERTISING is not even truly advertising. Every ad must have some "selling copy," even if only by implication. Anonymous ads—"congratulations from a friend," for instance—are actually charitable donations. These are acceptable but should be listed in roster of patrons. This not only saves space for more interesting editorial content but also gives better recognition and thanks to benefactors.

features, they are exercising an editorial right. But if they retain such copy only because "it's always been done" or for prejudices rather than for valid reasons, they aren't using their reasoning powers.

The first of these hardy perennials is the *quotation* that often accompanies each senior picture. We have already noted that here is danger of hurting a person by unseemly humor. An inappropriate phrase may be just as cutting. Most frequently these quotations are just plain stupid; the staff has settled on something less than definitive because it was too lazy or too unfamiliar with literature to be precise. In large schools, the staff may not be personally acquainted with each graduating senior and thus faces a task impossible before it is even begun.

Such quotations were used in early yearbooks to demonstrate the erudition of the staff, their familiarity with the classics. Today we take such knowledge for granted; to flaunt it is an affectation; to demonstrate ignorance thereof is ridiculous.

Class wills and class prophecies are far more often inept and banal than otherwise. As graduating classes increase in size, it becomes more diffi-

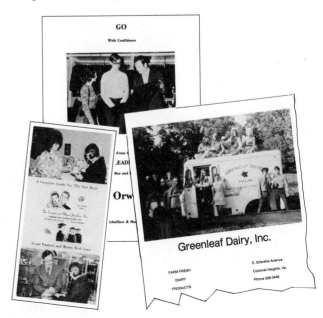

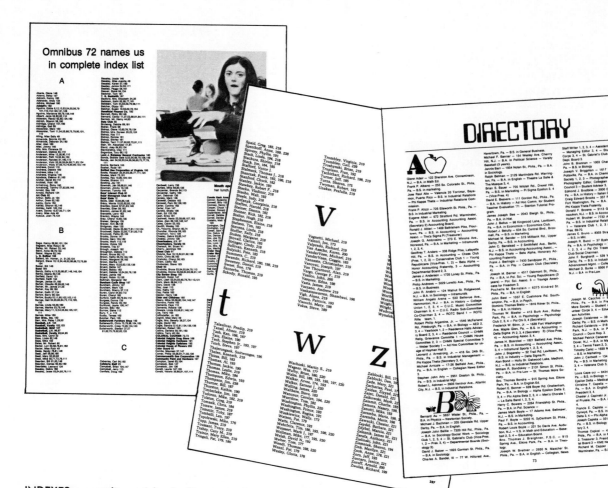

INDEXES are enlivened by both type and art. "Omnibus" uses same headline style and photo treatment as on other pages; advertisers' names are in boldface, no handicap when salesman calls on merchants next year!

In second example, large "tabulation letters" are used. In third, whimsical hand art (shown in actual size in fragment at right) makes pages interesting.

staff has enough of a job recording the past, without getting involved in the misty future.

For a democracy, America chooses an amazing number of Queens, and it's a rare high school that doesn't have a bevy of royalty. Most are overplayed by the typical yearbook. If the selection of a Queen is part of a Homecoming game or a Spring Festival, it must be reported, of course. But resist the temptation to overdo it. Pictures of pretty girls are always pleasant to work with. But we would hope that the contents of a yearbook would have a little significance as well as sheer eye appeal.

Many a yearbook staff picks a Hall of Fame, students who have made purportedly substantial contributions to the welfare of the school. Again, the staff takes on a job it should not. The staff should be the recorder, not the maker, of news. If a representative student group chooses a Hall, the book must record that. But the space devoted to such listings should be determined by the validity of the selections; too often they are made popu-

larity contests. Many a real contribution is made by the unsung worker; he should be recognized. Those students who customarily are chosen for Fame have usually received plenty of prior publicity.

If the yearbook staff consciously recognizes its functions, it will be able to evaluate these "honors" by their genuine value and present them appropriately.

Another waste of space is that given to baby pictures of students, especially seniors. It is no earthshaking revelation that babies look different from grown people. As soon as that fact is accepted, there is neither humor nor reason in running baby pictures. What can they possibly prove? And who cares?

The class history, in today's school, is an artificial chronicle. Rarely is the class a cohesive organization that even has a history; rarely does the class have a corporate personality. It is much more efficient to record the history of the whole school, as this is the viable organization in most instances.

Fads should be noted as part of the record of the school year. But the staff must remember that fads are—thank heavens!—short-lived. That means that the craze must be explained in words or pictures; a dozen years from now the reader's recollection of the fad will be so hazy it will mean nothing without full explanation.

Surely there is no place in a record as permanent as a yearbook for a collection of jokes and wisecracks. Rarely do these seem half as funny in print as they did six months ago when bandied about in the cafeteria. And those alleged witty observations that link students' names with those of musical recordings, comic strips, or current books grow stale so quickly that their odor permeates the whole book.

"Literary" Content

The 1970's saw the repeating of a cycle almost a hundred years old. When yearbooks—then called *annuals*—were new in America, they carried a lot of the material that we print today in our campus literary magazines. Essays, poems, and vignettes of fiction were a regular part of the yearbook at that time. A few staffs are using such material in their books today and adding to that a selection of "fine art"—drawings, paintings, etchings, and the like—which were not possible, for technical reasons, in early-American yearbooks.

Inserts or Supplements

An enduring problem for every yearbook staff is the coverage of spring events. If the book is to come out before the end of school, the final deadline must be in late winter or early spring. Many seasonal activities and, especially, commencement, baccalaureate, and year-end events, cannot be recorded.

The alternative is to have a book with a summer publication date, with a deadline just after the close of school. Because the printer works under far less pressure at that time, the lapse between final copy and delivery of books is considerably less than that for a spring publication.

Most schools dislike summer publication. The staff feels let down when there are few, if any, people around to applaud its work. To the student,

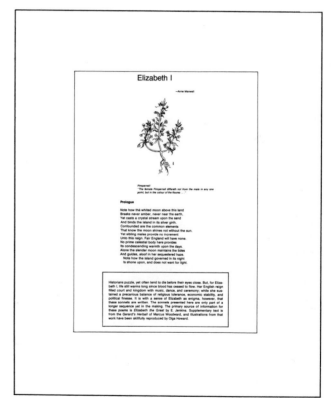

LITERARY PAGES, important part of earliest American yearbooks, are making comeback. Spread (left) has two poems with picture illustrating each, and separate photo. All pictures here face same direction and prevent editor from following axiom that "all pictures should face into page."

Single page (above) is from same book. It begins poem that takes four pages.

b.a. biology

BRIAN JOHN FLYNN
b.b.a. marketing
american marketing assn., intramurals in football, basketball, softball

ARTHUR FORMAN
b.b.a. marketing

BRUCE FORMAN
b.a. psychology
dean's list, peer teaching, pi gamma mu

BEVERLEY FORREST
b.a. drama-performance
homecoming queen, asst. director the crucible,
electra

STEPHEN FOSTER
b.s. art education
o.a.m. — treas., art club, newman club, dean's
list

JOHN FRAIOLI, JR.
b.s. engineering science

DAVID FRANKEL
b.a. history — secondary education

THOMAS FRATELLO
b.a. mathematics
delta tau, math club, intramurals

WILLIAM FRAZIER
b.b.a. finance
finance club, dean's list

ROCHELLE FREILICH
b.a. elementary education — english
chronicle

LYNNE FEIMOUR
b.a. psychology
floor rep., community action comm., softball
club

MICHAEL H. FRIED
b.b.a. finance
finance club — vice pres., veterans club

JUDITH FRIEDLAND
b.a. elementary education — social science
dean's list

DIANE FRIEDMAN
b.a. elementary education — american history

MARTIN FRIEDMAN
b.a. fine arts

PETER FRIEDMAN
b.a. psychology
hamlet, alpha psi omega, honorary drama society, drama productions

SUSAN FRIEDMAN
b.a. history

STAN FROELICH
b.s. socio-economics
o.r.s. — exec. comm., communications chm.,
floor rep., wvhc broadcaster, asst. tower e chm.

LINDA LEE FUCHS
b.a. fine arts
phi epsilon, nexus, o.r.s., art club, inter-sorority
council

DOROTHY ANN FURLONG
b.b.a. public accounting
accounting society

JUDY FURMAN
b.a. elementary education — social science
phi epsilon — corr. sec., s.e.a.n. y.s. — treas.

EDWARD R. GAFFNEY, JR.

F-G

samurai material arts club, hofstra vets, student
senate — vice pres., photo club

ANNE FILTON
b.a. elementary education — speech
dsd — hist., dean's list, speech honor society

EDWARD FINLAY
b.b.a. personal management
dean's list, honor society

LUCILLE FISCHER
b.a. sociology

RUSSELL FISHER
b.a. mathematics
math club — sec., dean's list, coalition of math
— vice pres., galois group

ROBERT FISHMAN
b.a. economics
dean's list, r.a., resident judiciary board —
assoc. chief justice, intramural football and basketball, big brother of america, sensitivity training

ELLEN FITERMAN
b.a. history
history club — sec., chronicle, freshman spon-

sor, homecoming

DOROTHY FITZGERALD
b.s. fine arts education
kappa pi, alpha sigma lambda

ROSALIE FLAMM
b.a. elementary education — sociology

PETER FLANNERY
b.a. english

JEFFREY FLAXMAN
b.b.a. management
r.a., dorm council, varsity tennis, undergrad.
asst., dorm social comm — chm., intramurals

PHYLLIS FLAXMAN
b.b.a. marketing
who's who (jr. college)

CARLA FLEISSNER
b.a. english

WANDA MARIE FLEMING
b.a. history
o.b.c., faculty comm., dean's list, delta sigma
theta — pres.

SUSAN FLINKSTROM
b.a. sociology
ivy bridge house, pi gamma mu, dean's list

STEPHEN FLUGER

100

SENIOR BIOGRAPHIES occupy two facing pages like this
one. On next two pages are only biographies. Such alterna-
tion prevents monotony of all-type or all-photo pages,
especially when graduating class is large one.

summer delivery is an anticlimax. The senior class has already begun to drift apart to jobs and perhaps summer college; there is no way that cherished autographs of classmates can feasibly be obtained. Summer distribution is not very convenient. Usually the school is torn up for summer cleaning and repairing. Faculty members are out of town; it is difficult to get responsible student help in distribution. With many students on vacation, that chore dangles along for too many days.

Postponing distribution to the opening of school in fall is a little better for students still in school. But, by the swift calendar of youth, a delay from May to September makes the book ancient history.

Thus most staffs wrestle with the problem of spring coverage.

An obvious solution is to cover one calendar year with a yearbook. If the deadline is March 1, the coverage goes back to the preceding March 1. But the rhythm of school life is geared to the academic, not the twelve-month year.

Underclassmen are not particularly disturbed by this system, which combines parts of two academic years. But the graduate has to buy next year's book to have coverage of his own school finale.

Of course, this system is better than that used by some schools. They just ignore spring activities. This is hardly logical. The record is incomplete by almost 25 percent, and the events of school-year-end are among the most colorful, significant, and memorable ones of a whole year, and, for seniors, of a whole high school career.

To pick up the record from the previous year at least prevents this serious gap in the continuing history of the school. Because of the strong similarity between the events of one year to the next, pictures of last year's commencement will stir almost as many memories as those of this year's. After all, there are few high-fashion changes in cap and gown or even in the setting and conduct of graduation exercises.

A good solution may be an *insert* or *supplement*.

This is an addition to the regular book, which is printed after the close of school and covers all the events of spring. The insert has a strong adhesive under a protective cover. This is peeled away, the insert is carefully placed within the covers of the book where it is fastened almost as securely as if it had been sewn there.

Inserts can be no larger than 16 pages; the cover must be made with enough extra room to accommodate it. Decision to use an insert—and its size—must be made before manufacturing of the cover begins, in midwinter.

There are problems with inserts, of course. Distribution has all the summertime woes already discussed. But because the *supplement* is relatively small, it is practical to mail it. Many yearbook printers will mail individual supplements directly from their plants. This saves time and effort, but the cost of envelopes and postage is an added burden that must be taken care of in the budget. Some schools mail the inserts to graduates and allow other students to pick it up after school resumes.

If mailing is done by the staff, arrangements must be made before the close of school for an adequate number of reliable workers and supervisors, for a suitable place to work, and for payment of postage.

The envelope carrying the insert must be plainly marked; too many people throw away mail without opening it. Clear instructions must be included so that the student knows how to make the insert an integral part of the book.

The insert must be right next to the cover. Although it can be at the front or back of the book, it is most logical to have it at the end.

There will be some loss of inserts. Some will

evaporate in the postal system; others will be wastebasketed in the student's home. Others will be misplaced before they are fastened into the covers. So it is wise to order more supplements than of the original book. Some advisers believe 1 or 2 percent is a sufficient overrun; others think 5 percent is more realistic.

After lost inserts have been replaced, any leftovers can be sold at the school the following autumn. In most instances, selling supplements at 25¢ will show a slight profit for the staff. Especially if you have good commencement pictures, many graduates will be happy to buy extra supplements to send to relatives and friends.

Often the staff will design the first page of the insert so that the 16-page unit becomes a self-sufficient book for just such use.

With either a summer-publication book or an insert, the main problem is meeting deadlines in those gloriously hectic days at the end of the school year or during those letdown weeks immediately afterward.

It is hard to keep a staff organized during the erosion of vacation activities. It is hard enough to discipline one's self to academic chores, without the need to meet a deadline delivery as implacable as the last day of school.

Yet these problems are not insoluble. Most of the insert copy can be written in advance. If there is a departure from plans, this will require only minor revision of copy.

Insert Photography

The editor should work closely with the photographer in planning photo coverage. The cameraman should shoot generously. After all, film is relatively the least costly of the ingredients in a photograph. Extra negatives are insurance against bad—but irreplaceable—shots; they also give the editor a wider selection to make layout work easier.

The editor should make his selections from the negatives. This saves the photographer the chores of making contact prints and of long darkroom duty.

Two people, an editor and a cameraman, can put out a 16-page insert in two weeks with no difficulty, especially when the pressure of classroom work has been lifted.

The extra effort required for a supplement is well repaid by the satisfaction of giving your readers—especially the seniors—a complete record of the academic year.

Portfolios

Another way of solving the end-of-the-year rush is use of the *portfolio technique*. In this method the yearbook is published in periodical sections. Each is the equivalent of a magazine, covering events for a chronological portion of the school year.

When the printer produces each "magazine," he prints twice as many copies as are needed for immediate distribution. Extra copies are stored.

When the final deadline arrives, the staff prepares the opening and seniors sections. Those extra copies of each of the magazines are gathered to create a book that is bound in the conventional manner.

Distributing production costs between a periodical and the yearbook reduces the price for which the staff must sell its book, and allows wider distribution.

A variation of this technique is to require the reader to keep each issue of the magazine. At the end of the year, he is given the final sections and a loose-leaf book cover into which he binds his accumulation of magazines. There is always danger that the typical reader will lose or misplace one or more of the sections and wind up with an incomplete book. But the staff can keep a few extra copies for such emergencies.

The cost of running a double quantity of portfolio sections—for immediate distribution and for later binding—is relatively low and assures each student a book complete without dog-ears, Coke stains, or mutilation. Even though loose-leaf covers can be as attractive as any other, they seem impermanent, and the reader doesn't respect the book as much as he would otherwise. It all adds up to the fact that permanently bound books are favored by most staffs.

Interestingly enough, those schools that have used the portfolio format report no major complaints from the student body that the final book is in a large part a duplication of previously published matter. The ability of even a small school to publish a substantial book in this manner seems to compensate for any lack of freshness of material.

Another method is to package the separate booklets in a *slip-box*, a five-sided container that is treated like a book jacket and into which the separate printed sections are placed with their spines showing.

Another variation of the portfolio format is to print pages on separate leaves and gather them, unsewn, into a shallow box. Sometimes sheets larger than the box are used and they may be folded in conventional or novel ways to fit. A daring staff may include things other than printed pages. When excavation for a new school uncovered a trove of fossil rock, one energetic staff dug through the slag piles to find several hundred fossils and placed one in each portfolio. Political campaign buttons, a piece of wood from a historic but now razed building, a dried leaf or flower, a phonograph record . . . the list of things that would stimulate memory is long. Students can be encouraged to use the box for their own memory box and to store in it their personal memorabilia . . . report cards, certificates, newspaper clippings, programs, invitations, and all the other ephemera we all love to collect, especially during our school years.

Although the potentials of a portfolio are exciting, it is necessary to note the debits on its ledger. Loose leaves are difficult to keep in order, even if folio numbers are printed on them. Thus the normal progression of a book is improbable or impossible; the editor never knows in what order the pages will be read.

Loose leaves are easily lost and get dog-eared just as readily. Sturdy and handsome boxes are as expensive as conventional book covers and in some cases cost even more. Easy and convenient fasteners are hard to find, and storage is inconve-

nient unless the box is made in a standard size to fit into a regular bookcase.

Official Records

The editor's search for excellence doesn't end when he sends the last copy to the printer or even when the book has been distributed to every student; the yearbook is one of the semiofficial records of the school and must be as accurate as is humanly possible.

It is absolutely amazing how many errors can sneak through, past eagle-eyed proofreaders. But, deeply as they are hidden in the proofs, errors flaunt themselves in the book. The staff should examine their book as minutely as possible. Each error should be reported to the editor at once. So should complaints by readers.

The editor should keep a written record of all errors and omissions. Then in four copies of the yearbook he should make necessary corrections, neatly and in India ink. One of these copies he keeps as his personal, perpetual reminder that accuracy is not easily come by. The second copy goes into the reference library of the future staff. The third goes to the school library and the fourth to the principal, with the request that he keep it among his official records.

PORTFOLIO FORMAT has several booklets packaged in box. Corner is removed from portfolio at left to provide easy access. Box at right has lithographed "cover." Both are standard size to fit into conventional book shelves.

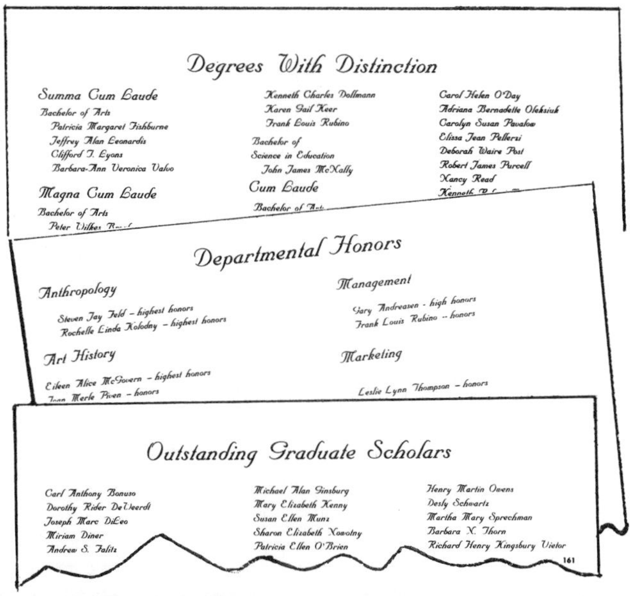

Degrees With Distinction

Summa Cum Laude

Bachelor of Arts
Patricia Margaret Fishburne
Jeffrey Alan Leonardis
Clifford T. Evans
Barbara-Ann Veronica Valvo

Magna Cum Laude
Bachelor of Arts
Peter Wilkes M...

Kenneth Charles Dallmann
Karen Gail Keer
Frank Louis Robino

Bachelor of
Science in Education
John James McNally

Cum Laude
Bachelor of Art...

Carol Helen O'Day
Adriana Bernadette Olekesiuk
Carolyn Susan Pavalow
Elissa Jean Pelkeri
Deborah Waire Post
Robert James Purcell
Nancy Read
Kenneth R...

Departmental Honors

Anthropology

Steven Jay Feld – highest honors
Rochelle Linda Kolodny – highest honors

Art History

Eileen Alice McGovern – highest honors
Joan Merle Pecen – honors

Management

Gary Andreasen - high honors
Frank Louis Robino .. honors

Marketing

Leslie Lynn Thompson – honors

Outstanding Graduate Scholars

Carl Anthony Bonura
Dorothy Rider DeUberdi
Joseph Marc DiEso
Miriam Diner
Andrew S. Falits

Michael Alan Ginsburg
Mary Elisabeth Kenny
Susan Ellen Muns
Sharon Elizabeth Nawotny
Patricia Ellen O'Brien

Henry Martin Owens
Derly Schwarts
Martha Mary Sprechman
Barbara X. Thorn
Richard Henry Kingsbury Vistor

ACADEMIC EXCELLENCE, primary concern of good school, is recorded on several pages (fragments of which are shown here) listing wide range of scholastic honors.

The reason for correcting the record is a compelling one. Suppose you were an employer and a young person applied for a job with your company. He tells you that he played the lead in the junior class play, and you think that such ability and training might be useful on the job. You stop off at the public library that evening and look up the applicant's yearbook. No listing there for his dramatic activities! Immediately you begin to wonder about his honesty.

Such incidents are not rare. School officials, asked to give references for former students, often refresh their memories by looking through a yearbook. Newspaper reporters use yearbooks as source material; so do the staffs of your student paper—and yearbook. Errors are often perpetuated beyond remedy by reprinting them.

There is a permanence to a book that gives it unusual credence and importance. A book is one of the most enduring monuments that any person can leave behind. A book deserves the most dedicated work that a staff can expend on it. And the satisfaction of a good book well repays that extra effort and devotion of the editor and staff.

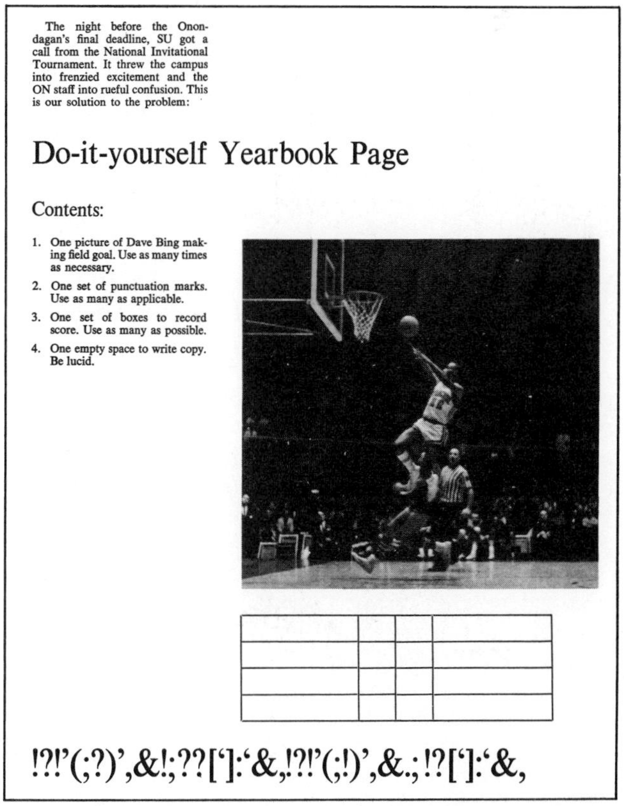

The night before the Onondagan's final deadline, SU got a call from the National Invitational Tournament. It threw the campus into frenzied excitement and the ON staff into rueful confusion. This is our solution to the problem:

Do-it-yourself Yearbook Page

Contents:

1. One picture of Dave Bing making field goal. Use as many times as necessary.
2. One set of punctuation marks. Use as many as applicable.
3. One set of boxes to record score. Use as many as possible.
4. One empty space to write copy. Be lucid.

!?!'(;?)',&!;??[']:'&,!?!'(;!)',&.;!?[']:'&,

IMPOSSIBLE DEADLINES arose when an invitational basketball tournament, highlight of athletic year, was scheduled to be played after yearbook was locked up. So this do-it-yourself page was printed. It contains action shot of team's leading scorer, blank scoreboard, assortment of punctuation marks, and empty space where owner of book could write about games. This technique can be used for any major event that occurs too late for inclusion in book.

Copy Writing

2

... The Heart of the Yearbook

You can have an excellent yearbook with no pictures; you cannot have a good book without words. With today's emphasis on yearbook pictures, written copy is often downgraded by the staff. But its importance cannot be overemphasized; words are essential in a book of record. Words give unity and cohesion to a book. Words create *readers*, whereas pictures too often attract only *lookers*.

Most of the area in a yearbook is devoted to pictures; that means that words must have exceptionally high quality because, by their very scarcity, they are conspicuous. The work of writers, copyreaders, and editors is vitally important. Like the diamond cutter, the copy staff works with objects small in quantity but high in importance.

The object of any written copy is, first and most important, to convey information. The writer is essentially a reporter. He must dig out the facts, then transmit them accurately and interestingly.

Accuracy is always the first essential of writing. The student assigned to a story, let us say, on the football season, must always go to the primary source. He must cover the games himself so that he can personally attest to the accuracy of his report. He must go to the official records of the team or athletic department, not trust to the reports printed in the newspaper. Too many inaccuracies have been perpetuated because a lazy reporter rewrote an account that contained some error. Of course, the newspaper reporter strove for absolute accuracy; but errors do creep into print, as all of us know all too well.

Editing and Proofreading

The writer has primary responsibility for accuracy. But so does everyone on the staff, and there are two important checkpoints at which reenforcements to the writer swing into action.

The first is the *copy editing* process. Its importance cannot be stressed too much, since the good editor can lift the quality of almost all copy.

The second is *proofreading*. This is a chore that is usually dreaded by student staffs. Admittedly it is painstaking and not at all glamorous. But the proofreader may console himself by considering that when Gutenberg invented printing as we now know it, some 525 years ago, the most learned, respected, and important person in the shop was the proofreader. He was the last authority to stamp the seal of accuracy onto a piece of printing. (He was—and is—also the only person in the whole intricate chain of graphic arts procedures who signs his name to his work. That's because it is so important, and he and his colleagues recognize this.)

Both these important staffers, *copyreader* and *proofreader*, use basically the same checklist. When they get copy from a writer or proofs from the typesetter, they check for:

1. Style

Does the copy follow the specifications of capitalization, spelling, abbreviations, use of symbols instead of words—1,2,3,4, $,¢,%, &—and other variables of choice that have been established for the book?

Has the printer set the type in the proper face, at the proper line lengths, with the correct leading? If there is a choice, has he used long or short descenders on the type, Modern or Old Style numbers, boldface or italics for the duplex?

2. Spelling of names

Of all the errors made in print, whether in newspaper, magazine, or yearbook, the one that exercises the reader most is the misspelling of his name. Jon Jones may not be quite sure whether you spell it "dillema" or "dilemma"; but he knows perfectly well he doesn't spell his name "John." To any person, his name is the most important word in the language; he expects everyone to treat it with proper respect.

Both copyreader and proofreader should have an authoritative list of names of all students and faculty members as well as other proper names that will appear frequently on their pages: "Punxatawney" High School, "North Western High," not "Northwestern"; "Mayor Smythe," not "Smith," for example.

Be particularly careful about names with unusual spacing. Is it "Mary Anne" or "Maryanne," "Van der Berg," "Vander Berg" or "Vanderberg"?

Our great national news magazines have a large staff of researchers who check every fact and the spelling of every word in a story. They put a penciled checkmark above each word to show that it has been tested for accuracy. This may be a little too much for the typical yearbook staff but the example is certainly one worth respecting.

3. *General Spelling*

The low level of spelling ability among students these days is the cause of lamentation by every editor. It is the result of inferior educational methods, and the poor speller is the victim rather than the culprit. But a poor speller knows that he is one and must take unusual pains to overcome his handicap. A dictionary should be on every desk in an editorial office and it should be the best used book in the house.

A concomitant of poor spelling is the *malapropism,* the use of a word that sounds similar to the correct one. In a report on a Student Council meeting, the writer said that "Jack Jones was elected by accumulation." He meant, of course, by "acclamation," and his ignorance was preserved for posterity. Unusual words should always be checked against the dictionary for spelling and meaning.

(In the forty-some years that this author has been writing, he has used the word "concomitant" approximately 857,396 times. He had to look it up in the dictionary 857,395 times . . . including just now. The one time he didn't, he spelled it wrong! No one is ever so experienced or so professional that he can ignore his dictionary. And correct spelling is the very first manifestation of the accuracy on which the journalist builds his career.)

4. *Correct information*

Here the copyreader must be a well-informed person who knows without having recourse to reference books that our team won the Central game by three points, not four; that it's Jim Jones, not Jack Jones, who is president of the Spanish Club; that the thoroughfare behind the school is Maple Avenue, not Street.

If he doesn't know, however—indeed, if there is the slightest doubt—the copy editor must bolster his own knowledge by checking primary sources. Thus he requires easy and constant access to a whole young library of reference material.

In proofreading, special care must be given to numbers. For 6 looks much like 8 or even 0; 3 and 8 get mixed up; so do 5 and 6 and, in some fonts, 1 and 7. Exert unusual care in checking tabulations such as athletic scores. In large masses, individual numbers tend to be overlooked . . . by the proofreader, that is, but not by the involved reader.

5. *Complete information*

The cub reporter, sent out on his first assignment, is cautioned to "Get the *five W's!*" If he does, his story will be complete. If he doesn't, there will be distressing holes in his narrative.

Who, what, where, when and why—or how.

These are the sacred W's and they must be fulfilled in yearbook copy, too.

The copyreader should studiedly use the list, consciously and conscientiously determining that each W has been answered. He should ask himself, "If I told this story at dinner tonight, would anyone in my family have any questions?" If they would, so will the reader.

"Why did Mitch Kramer leave the big game in the second quarter?"

"What was a dog doing in the chemistry lab, anyway, so that he got his tail in the sulfuric acid?"

"Was it Miss Smith, the French teacher, or Miss Smith, the math instructor, who was adviser to the Future Teachers?"

"You say the debate team had a 6–2 record but you list only seven schools they competed against."

A step-by-step checking will spot omissions that more casual reading may overlook.

In proofreading, make sure that all captions are on the page. With some editors rather capricious on when captions are or are not used, it is impossible to tell whether an omission is deliberate or inadvertent. (This is another reason that all pictures should carry a caption.)

In all captions, deliberately match up the name in the caption with the face in the photo. Too often only five names are given when there are six people in a picture. Or Ginny Brown, very obviously a girl, is identified as "at right" when that position is occupied by burly Mike Matthews, the heavyweight wrestler.

6. *Correctly numbered pages*

Loss or misplacement of a page of copy can create many difficulties; the copy editor should check this even before he starts reading. Some editors read the last line of a page and the first line of the succeeding one to make sure they run together. A missing page is particularly difficult to spot when a list of names is involved. It is so easy to skip a page and have "Michael VanAllen" instead of "Michael Thurber" and "Vanessa Van-Allen," because the intervening sheet, which began with "Thurber" and ended with "Vanessa," turned up missing.

In proofreading, this numbers checking is particularly important on those pages that do not have folios. This is usually the case when a picture bleeds into the area where the page number is ordinarily printed. In this case the proofreader must verify the page's position by checking numbers of adjacent ones.

7. *Typographic accuracy*

All humans make mistakes . . . even editors and printers! It's easy to hit the wrong key on a typewriter or a typesetting keyboard. Such errors are difficult to spot when the mistake creates a legitimate word. If we see "Xharles," we know at once that the typist was one key over for the "C" she wanted. And when we see "The fotbal teametaoin shrudlu" we know that the typesetter left a garbled line in the galley. But when a word is "of" instead of "or," "and" instead of "an," or "boy" instead of "bay," the scrutinizing eye is apt to pass right over the error.

Some typesetting machines can easily perpetrate transposition, "Christams" or "reenforcemnets." These are sneaky errors that often elude us.

Once the checker has found an error, he should read the next two lines with even greater care than usual: When we do seize upon a mistake, we feel so pleased with ourselves that we become overconfident.

The proofreader's job is to make sure that the typesetter has exactly duplicated the copy of the writer. If there has been an error in the copy that has been perpetuated in type, its correction is called an *author's alteration,* and this cost is charged to the yearbook. Such alterations—A.A.'s —that actually correct an error must be made, of course; we can't let the principal's middle initial be incorrect even if it does cost us a dollar to fix it.

But no editing should ever be done in type. If someone wrote about a "gray" sky above a football contest, and it went through all the editing processes, then the proofreader should not change it to a "glowering" sky just because that adjective seems more colorful to him.

Even in the editing process, where changes never cost money, the copyreader should be wary about changing words. It is the job of the editor to improve the copy by assuring its accuracy and, sometimes, by tightening it up. If a wrong word or phrase has been used, it must be corrected, of course. But after the editing process, the copy must still be that of the writer. Its original flavor must be preserved.

When a story is absolutely unusable for any reason—and often this is no reflection on the skill of the writer—it may be completely rewritten. Metropolitan newspapers have *rewrite men* who do nothing but this task. Few yearbooks, however, need such a specialist.

When a story needs rewriting, the original writer should first do so. The editor should explain in detail why the rewrite is called for. It may be that the story must be shortened—or sometimes even lengthened—more than normal editing can do. Perhaps a different *peg* is needed, the single element around which the study is written. Maybe the editor wants it in a lighter vein, to be rearranged, to be incorporated with another piece of copy.

It is more than just courtesy, it is good journalism to have the original writer do the rewrite, since he is familiar with the facts. If for any reason a second person rewrites an article, he should check it with the original writer: The new writer may get the wrong impression from a word or phrase and strengthen the misapprehension by stronger words or phrases.

In all instances, the original writer should be told why his piece has to be rewritten or why a new writer is going to be assigned to it. Not to do so will shatter staff morale and create far more, and more serious, problems.

The writer must tell his story concisely. Although space is always at a premium in any medium, this is especially true in yearbooks. Thus there is constant pressure to "keep it short!" Tight writing is difficult. The rambling writer is like the hunter who fires buckshot; if he uses enough of them, one must hit the target if only by accident. The tight writer shoots a rifle; he has only one bullet and he must put it precisely on target.

Fortunately, concise writing is usually the best writing. When you read your favorite author, notice how he has pruned away all excess words to retain only the functional skeleton of his writing.

Anyone can arbitrarily eliminate words. A classic example is of a newspaper cub reporter who wrote: John Jones, 35, looked up an elevator shaft to see if the elevator was coming. It was. Funeral Tuesday at 9.

The trick is to write in taut but interesting style that retains all important information.

It is not the function of this book to teach writing and composition; there are too many excellent books (and excellent teachers) on this subject that are already available to the yearbook staff. But it is never a waste to review fundamentals. The writer, like the athlete, must constantly practice the basics of his craft. You can't be a great football player if you can't make a simple tackle; you can't be a great writer if you haven't mastered the simple rules of grammar.

Organization of material is essential to interesting writing. The time spent in thinking about your material and outlining it—mentally and on paper —is as important as that in which you hit typewriter keys. Yearbook copy should be outlined in detail before writing begins.

Organization should be straightforward and simple. Straight chronological presentation will usually be easier for the reader to understand than complicated flashbacks.

Simplicity in sentence construction contributes to good writing style. Short sentences build readability; so do short paragraphs. Of course, there must be variety and contrast. A whole book written in brief, declarative sentences will soon become as painful as the Look-the-dog-runs content of first-grade reading lessons.

Simple words are usually more effective than long ones. It is exciting to learn and use new words; long new words have unusual appeal to the student who savors the fine flavor of our English language. But be resolute; vow that you will not use Mr. Roget's *Thesaurus* to replace short, crisp words with stuffy, polysyllabic phonograms.

Handbooks for writers constantly stress that adjectives should be treated warily, that strong verbs are more important than nouns. Taken with several grains of salt, these are valid admonitions. Use adjectives sparingly; the choice of the correct noun often eliminates the need for modifiers. Colorful verbs can describe the doer, the noun, as well as the action. Powerful verbs reduce the need for both adjectives and adverbs.

In any instance, however, be sure the word you choose is precisely the right one. The shading of meanings in the English language are many, subtle, and exact. A halfback may sprint, scuttle, scurry, flit, whisk, gallop, lope, stride, canter, race, spurt, dash, bound, spring, or just run. One of these words will give the exact meaning the writer seeks to convey; all others may be close but will be imprecise.

Often the writer can use allusion instead of definition. The simple phrase, *a David challenging Goliath*, says in four words by allusion what would take a long paragraph to explain by definition.

Be sure, however, that the allusions you use are enduring ones and not those of only brief life and passing interest. Do *The Vagabond Lover* and *Mr. Inside and Mr. Outside* mean anything to you or your friends? To your parents these were names packed with meaning, as they alluded to a popular singer and a pair of then-current football heroes. The names of the momentary idols of today will lose meaning just as rapidly—and we must always remind ourselves that we are writing for twenty years from now even more than for tomorrow morning.

Allusions to *Huckleberry Finn, a pound of flesh*, and *crossing the Delaware* (or *Rubicon*) do not age because they treat of the constant, the enduring things of life and common experience and reference. The Bible and Shakespeare won't lose meaning, because they treat of ageless topics rather than those of ephemeral interest.

A function of a yearbook is to conjure up memories for the reader long after he has left the scenes and years that the book records. A casual phrase, a wry wisecrack, the title of a song or book . . . all these can bring vivid recollections to the reader. Therefore we cannot edit out all topical allusions. But there should be an unobtrusive identification, so that the statement is not cryptic gibberish if the allusion isn't grasped. *The Ice Man* may immediately project an image of a basketball player who seemed coolest when the game was the hottest; it will not depreciate the allusion, but will make more sense to the person with faulty memory if we write instead, "The Ice Man—appropriate nickname for the imperturbable Center Johnny Grant—cooled off the invading Spartans."

Titles of songs are rich in connotation. There are few couples who do not react to "our song," and few individuals who are not pleased by even the first strains of a favorite melody. The skilled writer will often use musical titles to create a mood.

(It is interesting to note that some yearbook staffs include actual music—on records—with their yearbook. These usually include the Alma Mater and fight songs of the school; favorites, old and new, of the choir, glee club, band and orchestra, and pop tunes that came and went during the academic year. In large quantities, such records are relatively inexpensive; but for smaller schools the preparatory costs are too high to make the plan feasible.

(Inclusion of phonograph records in a yearbook has been the topic of heated argument ever since the first staff combined the media of sight and sound. The purists insist that a book is a written or visual record, that its staff has no business poaching in the area of audible communications. Proponents insist that a record is a record, whether it's on paper or on vinyl. If the function of a yearbook is to preserve and revive old memories, any technique is legitimate.

(The argument will probably never be settled to everyone's satisfaction. The answer will probably always be: You pays your money—if you have it—and you takes your choice. For us, this discussion of sound is of importance because music is so effectively connotative; the writer must strive to evoke just as many memories as melodies do, but with words alone.)

The writer must avoid two sins that are common to all communicators but are especially tempting—and deadly—to the teen-ager: *Purple prose* and *clichés*.

Purple writing is *overwriting*. It is the violation of the simplicity whose virtues we have already considered. It is pretentious—and ridiculous—like a girl wearing an evening gown for a gym class, or a quarterback directing: "As my audible instructions reach a volume of higher intensity, transmit the ovoid leather between your lower extremities into my digits," when all he really meant was: "Hike!"

Purple writing often employs clichés, although these shelf-worn phrases are bad enough all by themselves. Clichés were once fresh and colorful phrases. The writer who first said a man was "strong as an ox" or a child was "pure as the fallen snow" used the language well. The similes were apt, the phrasing rhythmic, the images imaginative. The phrases became clichés when overused and incorrectly used by people who were too lazy or too careless to create their own verbal images. The list of clichés grows longer daily, since each bright figure of speech—indeed, *anything* creative

—is immediately seized by the imitators. Phrases are repeated ad nauseam; a TV show about spies or doctors or detectives will spawn dozens of imitators; most popular music is patently imitative.

Two kinds of writing—humor and sentiment—are so delicate that missing perfection by even a slight margin can turn it into inedibility.

Written humor is always difficult to achieve. When an amateur comedian is clowning around with the gang at the soda shop, his witticisms are aided by the laughter and spirit of fun already there. The reader of written humor may be in anything but a receptive mood. The teen-party humorist can use gestures, grimaces and inflection to underline the point of his jokes; he may even retell one. For the writer, words alone must carry the whole burden of making the reader chuckle. The humor of a social gathering is appropriately fleeting; a joke perpetuated in written form too often grows moldy.

The greatest danger in humor, real or alleged, is that it is often cruel. Much humor is based on sadism and selfishness. We laugh at a pie in the face because it's a mild form of a fist to the nose; we howl with delight when a comedian slips on a banana peel . . . because we're so happy it isn't happening to us. Little humor in yearbooks is malicious, but it often cuts as deep as if its pain were intended. Teen-agers are especially sensitive and are most vulnerable to the careless word or the unthinking wisecrack.

The writer first, then the editor, must weigh all humor with especial care. They must lean over backward; if there is any danger, no matter how slight, that humor may hurt, throw it out.

There is justification—need, too—for sentiment in a yearbook. School years are sentimental years; an accurate record of such years cannot ignore sentiment. Overdone sentiment becomes maudlin, however, and the writer must remember that understatement here is far more effective than when "the lady doth protest too much."

If all advice to a young writer had to be condensed into one word, it would be simply: "Rewrite!"

Rewriting is hard work. The first draft for anything—whether for this book or a picture caption—usually comes easy. The writer is carried along by the excitement of creativity and the appeal of new material. The second draft comes much more slowly and with less pleasure. By the time an author has revised a paragraph a dozen times, it may be sheer drudgery. But rewriting is essential.

As you read the autobiography of any of the great writers, you will find that they all share the ability and the will to rewrite and rewrite, as many times as are required to come up with their "perfect" version. All true art requires self-discipline by the artist; his greatness is the reward for refusing to accept good-enough. The young writer who learns and accepts this lesson early in his career can be his era's Hemingway or Salinger.

A major advantage that the writer for a yearbook has over his counterpart on the newspaper or magazine is a little more time to polish up his copy. He should take full advantage of it by getting an early start on an assignment, then letting it stand for a few days before he goes back to the rewriting task.

All deadlines for the book should be established to take full advantage of all available time. The editor must insist that the writer use this time well; if assignments are going to be done at the very last moment, there will be no chance for the revisions that superior copy requires.

A yearbook is a single book. At least it is supposed to be. But often a yearbook is fragmented by violent change in grammatical and literary style between one section and another.

It is one of the most important jobs of the editor to give continuity and consistency to his book, to make it truly *one* book.

Editorial Style

A grammatical *style book* is an essential. How does the writer designate a certain group of students: Class of 1980, class of 1980, Class of '80, class of '80, Class of 80 or class of 80? Any of these forms is correct; none is wrong. Yet there must be consistency; if it's the "Class of 80" on one page and the "class of '80" two pages over, the reader is irritated and considers the book amateurish.

Many excellent style books are available to the student staff. Most scholastic press associations offer them at trifling costs. Associated Press and United Press International have excellent style books; so do all metropolitan newspapers. Perhaps the printer of your yearbook has such a booklet available to you.

It is not too big a job to draw up your own style book. If your school already has a style book, do not make changes on whim or whimsy. Continuity from year to year is almost as important as that from page to page. It is annoying and confusing to a staffer if style changes each year he works on the book.

A style book should pay particular attention to capitalization. There are two basic styles, *up* and *down*. In *upstyle*, capitalization is done generously: the Latin Club, Class of '81, Mr. John H. Jones, Class Adviser. In *downstyle*, only the distinctive words in a title and only those in a specific title, are capped: the Latin club, class of '81, Mr. Jones, class adviser.

Downstyle is often abused by eliminating all capitals, especially in headlines. This is disconcerting to the reader and is insulting to the person or organization so referred to. The poet e. e. cummings made a pleasant gimmick of spelling his name without caps. But no editor has the right to spell a person's name with all lowercase; he is a specific, a unique individual, a proper noun. To downgrade a proper name into a common noun is insulting.

Rules of usage, which every good writer follows, call for proper nouns and the first word in a sentence to be capitalized. To ignore these rules is to demonstrate ignorance or bad taste.

Rules for capitalization should be clearly stated, and examples must be numerous.

Misuse of abbreviations can be tricky. Abbreviations should be used only as part of a closely knit phrase, never as a free-standing word. You would abbreviate in "Main St." but not in "he walked down the street." Titles are abbreviated when used with a name: "Dr. James Brown," but not otherwise, as "Mr. Brown, a doctor of philosophy from Harvard"; "Principal Albert T. Hughes" or "Coach Jerry O'Neill," otherwise "Mr. Albert T. Hughes, principal," or "Mr. Jerry O'Neill, coach."

These examples call attention to a problem unique to scholastic publications, the differentiation between students and teachers or other adults. Normally this is done by referring to all adults as Mr., Miss, or Mrs. Some staffs are using the new "Ms." but they may be rushing into territory scary even to angels. Some women are insistent that they be designated as Ms. But an impressive number of polls show that the great majority prefer the traditional titles. A staff cannot be faulted if they use Miss and Mrs. (In case of doubt about marital status, it is socially correct to refer to a professional woman as Miss.) But it is considered less than totally couth to label a woman Ms. when she detests that title. Therefore, for the sake of peace of mind, it may be best to stick to the accepted polite forms. The first time the name is used, it is given completely: "Mr. John H. Jones, Miss Kathleen Brown." Thereafter, the person is referred to as "Mr. Jones" or "Miss Brown." Students are referred to as "John Jones" or "Mary Black" the first time and then as "John" or "Mary." Note that this is contrary to usage by professional publications; they do not use Mr. with a complete name and, often, they will use only the last name for repeated usage. If you use a professional style book, be sure the necessary correction is made in this area.

Proper reference to clergymen is essential as a mark of respect, not only to the man but to his church. The most used term is "Reverend" or "Rev."; it must always be accompanied by "the." The first reference is to "the Rev. William P. Gordon," thereafter to "the Rev. Mr. Gordon." If the clergyman has an academic degree, he is first identified as "the Rev. Dr. William L. Norriss," thereafter as "Dr. Norriss."

Organizations must be identified *in full* the first time, "Young Men's Christian Association" or "Parent-Teachers Association," even if they are more familarly known by their abbreviations. When those abbreviations are used, the periods are dropped: "YMCA, PTA, UN," etc.

Punctuation in body copy is that of conventional grammar.

So is punctuation in *headlines*, although the semicolon is used instead of a period. Any punctuation in a head, except a question mark, usually weakens the headline, and the writer should seek to avoid the need, even for commas.

The handling of *type* that accompanies a picture must be in a style adopted by the staff; there is no universal reference book to consult. This is discussed in detail in Chapter 3 because it becomes a typographical problem as well as an editorial one.

The customary rules of grammar and usage apply in other categories. Newspaper style is usually followed in the use of numbers. Numbers below 10 are spelled out. Figures are used for street numbers, time or day, percentages, and sports scores. Figures that begin a sentence are always spelled out.

A specific dictionary and edition thereof should be picked as the final arbiter for spelling. If one writer spells it "advisor" and the other, "adviser," both can cite authority of recognized dictionaries. It is the responsibility of the editor to make sure that everyone on the staff has a common reference. The "official" dictionary must, of course, be available in the yearbook office at all times.

Copy Preparation

Although not strictly a matter of style, the handling of copy is usually specified in the style book. Almost always, the rules will call for copy typewritten *double space*, on *one side* of unlined 8½″ × 11″ paper, either bond or newsprint.

Each piece of paper must be *slugged*. Usually identification includes the slug line such as LATIN CLUB or FOOTBALL; the name of the writer, and the date (either of submission or when due):

FOOTBALL
Bill Smith
Oct. 12

If the story runs more than one page, the first page has MORE typed or written at the bottom. The second sheet is identified:

—2—
FOOTBALL
Bill Smith

The end of a story is always plainly marked with a *30-mark*: XXX, END,—30—,——0——or a similar device.

Always make carbon copies of any material,

FOOTBALL
Billy VanDemand
12/5/73

1 of 3
55 lines

during commencement ceremonies in the stadium last M

It was a good football season.
It wasn't a great one; Western came in third in the 10-team Midstate Conference. But we did beat our traditional rival, Central, in an 11-2 thriller. Jack Cline was named to the All-State second team as a defensive tackle. And school spirit was high.
All attendance records for the Alumni Memrial Stadium were shattered. The Homecoming pep rally was so large it overflowed LaFayette Square. And when Tug O'Leary intercepted a Valley pass and galloped 93 yards for a touchdown, there was no device known to mankind that could have measured the decibels of delerious screams..... even though it was obvious that we couldn't snatch a victory in those closing minutes.
Blue-and-Gold fans were perhaps too optimistic before the season started. Then ---the days before practice officially began--- George "Gipper" McNeil, the team's leading runner last season, broke his leg in a bike accident. Coach Robert Falson shuffled his veterans to fill the gap. We lost the first game, to Capital, 30-6, and the next to Clearwater, 9-6.
But then the sophomore line ---six were second-year students--- began to click. Their brilliant play

(more)

DRAMA CLUB
Sue Mischiewski
Nov. 12 '73

Copyread by JBC 12-14-73

The student dramatists at Waldhaven put on a very unique series of 1-act plays as part of the summer recreational program, and then they kept right on when school began.
Only two weeks after classes started up, they presented "The Fur-Lined Sports Car" at both senior and junior assemblies. John "The Actor" Buffano was just fabulous as he took five curtain calls for his outstanding performance.
In co-operation with the music department, dramatics students staged "The Music Man" early in November. This was the first musical that has ever been staged at WHS, and it was a huge success. Mr. John G.C. Benetto, the dramatics coach, and Mrs. Carol Fuller, music director, were lavish with their praise, not only for the cast, but for the unseen members of the production crew.
"Manny Welner, the Music Man, and Virginia Del Porto, Madame Librarian, were excellent," said Mr. Benetto. "But I think Randy Duchamps's work as head of the set-building crew was just as outstanding.
The audience seemed to agree. For when the railroad coach, which is the setting for the first scene, was split apart and hauled off the stage, the audience gave a spontaneous cheer. And the library set was greeted by the same amount of applause just as soon as the curtain was lifted.
But it was the familiar music ---"76 Trombones", the love duets and "You Gotta Know the Territory"--- that obviously delighted an audience that set a new record for attendance for any student production.
.....MORE.... MORE .... MORE...MORE

FIRST DRAFT OF ARTICLE is "slugged" in top-left corner with section or topic, writer's name, and date submitted. Notation in top-right corner shows that there are three pages; if one gets lost, search can begin immediately. First type line has been copied from sample of set type at desired width to make it easier to estimate length of copy required. Ordinarily this line would be X-ed out. Or it would be typed on scrap paper and margin stops of typewriter set to that length.

and at *every* stage of rewriting. Copy does get lost; it will save panic to have a carbon on hand when the inevitable happens. If copy goes through much revision, it often can assure accuracy to compare various carbons.

Copy Control

Copy control is essential for yearbook writing. Space allotted for a story is rigidly defined, and copy must be written to conform to that space. There is usually no adjacent column or page onto which an over-long story can be jumped.

Many yearbook printers furnish *copy sheets* on which the finished story is typed. Vertical lines, printed in light ink, indicate how wide the typewritten line must be to equal a line of type in the book. Here adjustments are made for different

COPYREAD ARTICLE has been tightened by deleting redundant words. Coach's name has been corrected by changing middle initial, and consistent style has been given titles of dramatic productions. Note that *More* at bottom of page alerts editor to successive pages. Copy editor has signed name.

type sizes and line lengths.

If the printer doesn't furnish such sheets, it is easy to set up your own specifications. Your printer will furnish you with sample blocks of your body type. Now assume that you want to write enough copy to fill an area that the dummy shows as 20 picas wide and 3½ inches deep. On the sample type block, measure several lines 20 picas wide and, by counting, determine the average number of characters per line. Set your typewriter margins so you type lines with this many characters. On the sample block, measure 3½ inches vertically to determine how many lines of type will fit into your available space. Now write as many lines as are required, typing each as full as possible without excessive hyphenation.

This writing-to-space method works out quite well but can never be perfectly exact because, on your typewriter, each character occupies the same space, be it a fat M or W or a skinny 1 or i. In the

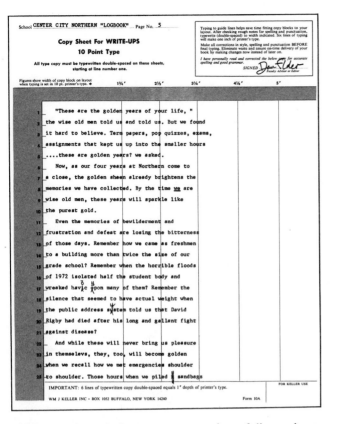

FINAL COPY, ready for printer, is typed carefully on sheets provided by publishing firm. Typing errors have been corrected, and exact number of lines are recorded in copy log so that layout man can provide proper space in dummy.

As many printers do today, this one requires signature of editor or adviser, noting that "I have personally read and corrected the below copy for accurate spelling and good grammar." Implicit is that signer has checked for accuracy of fact and for standards of good taste. Often immature staffers have created great embarrassment—and sometimes financial damages—for staff and school by bypassing adviser and sending copy of dubious taste directly to printer. System shown here eliminates such irresponsible short-circuiting.

typesetting process, each character gets only as much space as it needs. Thus the typewritten line with many narrow characters will not make a full line of type. Necessary adjustments will be minor, however, and can be done on the galley proofs.

Widows

Many editors insist that all type blocks, stories, or picture captions, be written so that the last line is full. This may make a neat looking page but it is philosophically unsound. The function of type is to convey information, not to make neat rectangles. If the copy has been properly written, it should not be revised just to "kill a widow." (A *widow* is that very short line of type at the end of a paragraph.)

No editor would think of rewriting the Gettysburg Address to kill a widow. Although the aver-

age copy for the average yearbook may not have quite the literary perfection of Abraham Lincoln's, it should not be rewritten for purely mechanical reasons, either. (Typographic aspects of widows are discussed in the next chapter.)

Flowing Copy

The presentation of written copy is a matter of basic policy that the editor and staff must set very early in the planning stages.

The book should be so arranged that there will be copy very close to the opening pages. This sets the general tone for the whole book and usually introduces and explains the theme. Although pictures compel attention and draw the reader immediately, the book doesn't really "start" before the first written copy.

Quality of written copy can be raised markedly by adopting the technique of *flowing copy*.

In the typical yearbook, copy is written on a page-by-page basis. A page or a spread is given to each club or to each game on the football schedule. Verbal copy is written to fit available space. This often results in a constricting situation. If the available pictures are many and good, there will be little room for type. Therefore the writer must give only cursory treatment, no matter how important the subject. On the other hand, when there are few pictures available, the writer may have to pad out inconsequential matter just to fill up the space.

The *flowing-copy* technique remedies this situation. Copy is written for a whole section, rather than on a page-by-page basis. Now the editor has a running narrative that covers the whole basketball season, let's say. He places type where it will help make an attractive page. If there are no (or few) good pictures of the Central City game, he need not fill a whole spread with that game. Or, if the traditional game with North High produced many good pictures, they need not be confined to a single spread. The same flexibility allows him to place type where it will be most pleasing and not just where it will fit. Freed from arbitrary space restrictions, the writer can write more smoothly and logically.

Whether flowing or page-by-page copy is used, the records of all competitive teams—athletic or academic—should be listed in a simple box-score tabulation. When, in later years, the reader wants to find out how your school did against its traditional rivals in basketball, he ought to be able to find out by referring to a single table rather than having to wade through the entire narrative copy.

The constant criterion of a good book is that it be "in good taste." The term resists definition, as taste is often a symptom of the age in which it is acceptable.

But there are a few topics upon which cultured people over the past several centuries have

"FLOWING COPY" tells story of graduates' four years at school. In this book, large 18-point type was used with generous areas of white space. Note how huge, "8-line initial" accents page. Forty-two pages at beginning of book were devoted to this running copy.

HAT is a university? More than buildings, faculty, syllabi and even students. What is Syracuse University? More than a constantly expanding complex of buildings on Piety Hill. More than a roster of distinguished scholars. More than fifteen thousand students . . . even more than a nationally known football team.

A university becomes a whole far greater than the sum of its parts. It becomes a being of its own, with personality, will and aspiration, peculiar and unique. It becomes a living organism finding its strength and soul from a unique alloy of many diverse and disparate entities.

Each of us is part of this Syracuse University. Each retains his individuality, wrestles with his own problems, seeks his own goals. Yet each of us loses part of himself to this "universe" of which he is a part. From this he gains strength even as he gives it.

From the diversity of its components a university gains a unity all its own.

Unity through diversity makes Syracuse University what it is today.

Just what it is today has never been articulated; perhaps it never can be. All we can do is define its components and sense the whole that coalesces from them.

For this mystic entity, which we call our university, can never be seen in its entirety any more than we on a small planet, called Earth, can see all of the universe in which our globe orbits.

Its parts can be seen. And the *Onondagan* presents to you some of the tangibles of an intangible whole.

Each of us will see even these parts differently. The image our eye carries off these pages will be tinted with our own memories, with our own awareness, within the context of our years on the Hill in which the events recorded here have their own diversity of significance, of interpretation, of retention.

Let's tour this piece of geography — the physical Syracuse University.

enter the young —
a peaceful
occasion?
war cannot mar
a person's right to
personal beliefs

FLOWING COPY can be brief, like this. Each spread has a large photo and small copy block that expand upon theme, "Enter the Young." Or . . .

The point of it all is out there

Barry Rothman

Jonathan Royce

Bobbi Schweitzer

Ann Rutecki

Mary Scibetta

a little beyond that last rise

you can just barely see, hazy and purple on the sky.

And who, disguised as Clark Kent, mild . . . Mo Curran.

Clay Stahlka

Stephen Starkweather

Sandra Stearns

. . . Steblin

"RUNNING HEADS" resemble running copy in that they carry verbal message from page to page to page. Examples here are all right-hand pages. But running heads may appear on either or both pages of spread. Each spread requires at least one such head, however. If full-page photo breaks into such head, it should be placed between sentences.

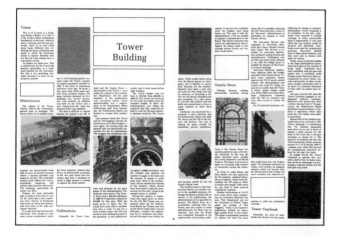

. . . FLOWING COPY can be as long as this, which goes on for eight pages in newspaper-column form. Rectangles of halftone, black, gray, or white are visual devices that carry continuity through several sections like this one.

FOOTE & DAVIES, INC.
POST OFFICE BOX 13084 · ATLANTA 24, GEORGIA
764 MIAMI CIRCLE, N. E. · PHONE CEDAR 7-1611

Page Sequence Plan   FORM 17

TO BE PREPARED BY THE EDITORIAL STAFF

Publication _LOGBOOK_   Date _1—_
School _northern H.S_   _Center City_   _USA_
(name) (city) (state)
Page Size _9X12_   No. of Pages _160_   Stock _TEXTWITE_
End Sheets _Blue with art_   Dividers _regular stock_
2nd Color _ORANGE_ (color)   On Pages
Process Illustrations _none_   On Pages

PAGE NUMBER (LEFT / RIGHT)	SUBJECT	Large Pix	Large Art	Med. Pix	Med. Art	Small Pix	Small Art	Total Pix	Total Art	TEXT	HEADS Main	HEADS Sub	SPECIAL INSTRUCTIONS
17	Campus Scenes			1	1	2		3	1	✓			Duotone on NOOK
18	Shop Street	1						1		✓			
19	" "				1	2		2	1	✓			
20	Fall (full page)	1						1					Duotone bleed top
21	Text "4 yrs"		1						1	×	×		Initial in color
22	"					1		1		×		×	
23	Winter (full)	1						1					
24 / 25	DIVIDER ACTIVITIES	①						①			×		Orange tint block reverse ½ tone
26	Student Senate			1		1		2		✓	×		
27	Joint Court			1		1		2		✓	×		
28	Dorm Council					2		2		✓	×		
29	Full page pic N-Day	1						1					duotone 4 bleeds
30	Goon Squad			1		2		3		✓	×		
31	" "					3		3		✓		×	
32	Text "we start					1		1		×	×		Initials in color
33	"					1		1		×		×	"NO color"
34	A.D.S.	1						1		×			
35								2					

COPY CONTROL is necessary to meet deadlines without panic or all-nighters. On this chart, pages for two "signatures" are listed. Because whole signature must be in printer's hands before he can do much of work, it is more important to send complete 16-page signature than to send greater number of pages scattered among several sigs.

A YEARBOOK PROGRESS CHART
that editors find helpful in checking the work of PRODUCTION

Page No.	Page Description	Copy Assigned to	Copy Due	Copy Sent to Printer	Drawing or Photo Assigned to	Drawing or Photo Due	Drawing or Photo Sent to Engraver	Page Completed
17	Science	Mark	11/1	11/7	(a) Dan (b) Ted	9/15	11/7	
18	" Full-pg pic		11/2	11/7	Dan	9/20	"	
19	Math	Sue	11/2		Ted	10/2	11/7	
20	"	"	"		"	"	"	X
21	"	"	"		"	"	"	X
22	"	"	"	11/7	"	"	"	X
23	Dist. Ed	Mona	10/28	11/7	Bill	10/2	11/7	X
24	"	"	"		"	"	"	X
25	Special Arts	Fred	11/1	11/7	Bill	10/8	11/7	X
26	"	"	"	"	"	"	4	X
27	Home Ec	Vera	11/2	11/7	Ted	10/9	11/7	X
28	2 page pic 4 bleeds			11/5	Dan - Photo	11/6		
29					Bev - art			
30	Music	Trina	10/27	11/7	Dan	10/8	11/7	X
31	"				"	"	"	X
32	Phys Ed	Joe	11/1		Ted	10/19	11/7	X

COPY CONTROL begins with assignment sheet. Some editors ask writer or photographer to initial in the third or sixth column of form like this to show acceptance. Absence of X in final column alerts editor to missing page so he can begin remedial action.

agreed. They believe that certain details of plumbing, domiciliary or physiological, are not discussed in company that you respect. They believe that certain human activities gain dignity and meaning in intimacy and that they should not be conducted in public places . . . or in public print. They believe that certain references to race, creed, or color are offensive . . . to a listener or reader as well as to the direct subject of such bigotry. They believe the name of the Deity—no matter what the specific word—is so sacred to so many people that it should not be used as cheap slang.

This common decency is no handicap to the communicator, be he writer, photographer, or editor. Writers and artists have "told it like it is" for generations without resorting to gutter jargon. Truth, frankness, realism, strong commitments . . . none of these is a monopoly of the current world. And none of them is license for a foul vocabulary.

Good taste also prohibits some language that may not even be obscene or vulgar. It is a hallmark that "A gentleman never embarrasses anyone around him." An excellent paraphrase is that a good editor does not do so either.

If a student editor would not read copy aloud to his mother or grandmother, if he would not use such language to a person for whom he has great respect or affection, if he would not show, face to face, a humiliating picture or paragraph to the butt of the joke, then such material ought to go into the wastebasket.

In the few short years that have gone by since the Dirty Speech Movement at Berkeley, many of the most foulmouthed of those demonstrators have acknowledged the embarrassment they suffer today because of their lack of common courtesy, then, to their listeners. A yearbook will be around for a long time. The wise editor wants it to be a memento of his best efforts, not of a show-off little kid who scrawls nasty words in chalk on the front sidewalk. Chalk eventually wears off; printer's ink is permanent.

The day a yearbook is distributed, written copy is nonessential; the reader is well satisfied by the pictures. But once he has skimmed through the photographs, he wants copy; a book has traditionally been a book of words. As the years pass, words become far more important. Memory dulls; a picture that needed no caption a month after it was taken becomes almost meaningless a dozen years later, unless words refresh memory.

The wise editor knows he is producing a book whose value should increase with years, so he recognizes the importance of good written copy and insists that his staff produce it.

MASTER CONTROL CHART for ROY

Page No.	Page Contents (Itemize)	Editor Assigned	Copy due	Typed Copy rec'd	Copy checked (Initial)	To Printer	Art—Assigned to specify it (photos, drawings)	Identify itemize	Art due	Art rec'd	Art to Printer	Page Complete	Page Proofs Received	Page Proofs OK back to Printer
33	FACULTY	Gloria	10/30	11/4	BG		Photo	3	10/15	10/12			11-21	11-23
34	"	"		11/4	BG		"	1		10/10			"	
35	"	"		11/5	BG		"	4		10/17				
36	FULL-PAGE ART DRAWING						Mark	1	10/27	10/27	10/28		11/20	11/22
37	Curriculum	Bill T.	10/27	10/25	BT		Photo	2	10/15	10/12			11-21	11/24
38	Language	"	"	"	BT		"	5		10/12				
39	"	"	"	"	BT		"	1		10/10			"	11/25
40	" Latin	"	"	10/27	BT		" +Hand	1/1	10/12	10/12				
41	" Spa.	Sue	10/26	10/25	Sm		Photo	2	10/12	10/12			11-22	"
42	" Lit.	Dolly	10/26	10/27	Bru		"	2		10/12				
43	MATH	Jim	10/27	10/26			" +Hand	2/1	10/12	10/10			11-23	11/26
44	"			10/27			"	1	3/1	10/12			
45	"			10/28			Photo	2	10/11				
46	SCIENCE	Allan	10/25	10/25			"	2	10/11				
48	HISTORY			10/27									

WALL CHART shows progress of editorial staff's work. Written copy is listed on left of chart, artwork on right. Note ingenious system in third-from-last column. Rectangle is divided into four quarters by an X. When written copy is complete, right-hand triangle is blacked in as for pages 33–35. When art is finished, left triangle is filled as for page 36. Blacked bottom triangle (as for page 39) indicates that dummies have been drawn. When page is packaged for printer, final square is filled in as for 42–43. Editor can quickly spot pages that are delayed and remedy omissions.

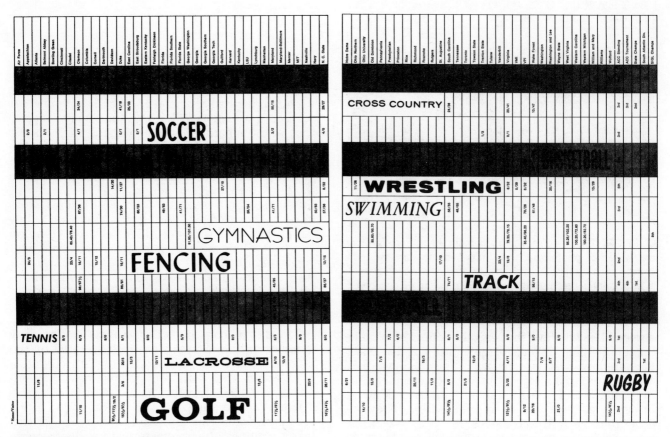

SEASON SPORTS RECORDS list every athletic contest—major or minor—in convenient and interesting form. Spread at right is part of five-page section. Bouncing ball changes appropriately.

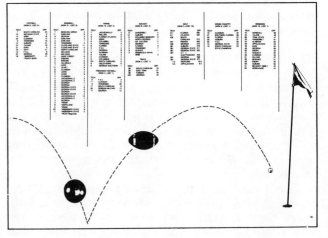

WHOLE ATHLETIC YEAR is summarized in attractive two-page charts. Numbers in top right indicate team standing in conference competition. Football team, for instance, was champion; basketball, fourth.

Varsity Football

A spark
ignites an explosion

Kneeling: Larry Holsey (Most Valuable Player, off., co-captain), *Front Row:* Tim Landrum (Unsung Hero on def.), Robert Jackson (Best def. back), Rom Williams (Best def. lineman), Joe Reynolds (Most Valuable Player, def., co-captain, W[N] spark Plug Award), Shannon Miller (Sidney Friend scholar-athletic award). *Top Row:* Chris Brooks (Unsung Hero, off.), Butch Anthony (Best off. back), Joe Basco (Most improved on def.), Des Hamilton (Best off. lineman), Alex Thomson (Most improved off.).

Football Scoreboard			
Fletcher	vs.	Stanton	41-21
Fletcher	vs.	Jackson	16-14
Fletcher	vs.	Lee	14-13
Fletcher	vs.	Raines	7-21
Fletcher	vs.	Forrest	25-18
Fletcher	vs.	Englewood	0-20
Fletcher	vs.	Ribault	21-14
Fletcher	vs.	Wolfson	27-0
Fletcher	vs.	Paxon	21-22
Fletcher	vs.	Parker	41-28

Upper Middle: The Senators break onto the field with explosive spirit echoed from all sides. *Upper Right:* Carried off the ground, Coach Poppell reflects the rewards of dedication. *Lower Right:* Brothers in purple, Robert Jackson and Marion Russ lock the door of escape for a Fletcher foe. *Lower Middle:* Butch Anthony's sinews stretch skyward in search of leather. *Lower Left:* Coach McCann and Coach Scott respond joyously to Tim Morgan's successful use of the many skills they have taught.

SEASON RECORD in particular sport appears on **gray panel**. Report is given in copy as well. Scores are essential and are best given in this tabulated form.

WOMEN'S SPORTS AND INTRAMURALS, both consistently ignored in typical yearbooks, are properly reported here. Yearbook cannot be complete history of school year if it ignores these two activities, which usually involve many more students than do varsity sports.

Women's Intramurals

Overall Winners

First Place—Independents

Second Place—Alpha Sigma Alpha

Third Place—Hickman Hall

Outstanding Individual

Carol Henderson, Independents

Outstanding Manager

Susan Ferry, Roberts Hall

Sportsmanship Award

Roberts Hall

Tennis Singles

First Place

Susie Grafton, Jones Hall

Second Place

Sue Beach, Independents

Tennis Doubles

First Place

Carol Henderson,
Suzanne Dees—
Independents

Second Place

Kay Jackson,
Linda Sparks—
Independents

Type
3
... *Yeoman of the Yearbook*

The function of a yearbook is to preserve and convey information. While much of this job is carried by photography, the essential information is that which is carried by type. In the past two decades less and less space in a yearbook has been occupied by type; the type that is used must therefore carry a bigger burden of communication.

For that reason, the selection of type is extremely important. To make it intelligently requires at least a basic knowledge of type and typography.

Typography is a vast, complex, and fascinating art. People have devoted a pleasant lifetime to its mastery. The student editor doesn't have time to get a master's degree; he needs a brief cram course in the subject.

Even a cursory inspection of magazines, newspapers, and yearbooks makes believable the fact that there are thousands of variations of typefaces. But by grouping them into a few basic categories or races, it is comparatively easy to acquire enough knowledge to use type well.

Classifications of Type

The most widely used type race is *Roman*. Yes, it was developed in ancient Rome. Its characteristics are the thinning and swelling of curved strokes and comparatively thin horizontal lines with thick vertical ones. Romans have *serifs*, little finishing lines at the end of regular strokes.

Oldstyle Romans have heavy, *bracketed serifs*, joined to the main stroke by curves; the difference between thick and thin strokes is minimal.

Modern Romans have straight, thin, and unbracketed serifs, and the contrast between thicks and thins is marked.

Even our familiar Arabic numerals come in two styles. Modern numbers are all the same height; Old Style numbers are designed with 3, 4, 5, 7 and 9 extending below the baseline. The numbers in this paragraph are Modern.

Italics are Romans that slant to the right. They have thicks and thins and serifs, either in Old or Modern styles. Sometimes a little flicking curve, a *finial,* is used instead of serifs. Technically, only Romans have an Italic as a slanted form; letters of other races that slant to the right are correctly called *Oblique* but in common usage are more often—if incorrectly—also referred to as Italic.

In the printer's language, just plain "Italic" means a Roman Italic; when the term is used to denote the slanting form of another race, it is used in combination with the racial name, as Sans Serifs Italic.

Numbers and *special characters* such as $ and & are designed in both the perpendicular and oblique forms.

Roman Italics often have *Swash* letters with decorative flourish-strokes that give an aura of elegance to a headline. They have a close kinship with the *Written* letters, as the original Italic design was based on handwriting.

The oldest form of metal type is *Text* or *Black Letter.* This is commonly called *Old English.* (This usage is incorrect, however. To call all Text letters Old English is like calling all automobiles Chevrolets!) In this letter form, curves have been changed to straight lines. It is comparatively narrow and dark and gives a distinct feeling of pomp and ceremony. It is frequently used for official anouncements or church printing. In yearbooks it is used rarely, mostly for *In Memoriam,* although it would be appropriate for headlines if the theme were *When Knighthood Was in Flower* or the Renaissance.

Sans Serifs and *Gothics* make another race. They are monotonal; every stroke—horizontal, vertical or diagonal—is of the same weight. They have no serifs; (sans is French for "without"). The Gothics are generally narrower and blacker and their curves are not as graceful as those of the Sans. Both—but especially the Sans Serifs—are widely used in yearbooks.

Square Serifs are also monotonal. They have serifs but these are no fine little lines; they are as heavy, and sometimes heavier, than the main strokes. If the serifs are just as heavy as the main strokes, we call the letter an *Egyptian Square.* If the serif is heavier than the main stroke, the letter is an *American Square.* The Squares tend to be rather heavy; but there are light versions that are pleasant for yearbook use. American Squares have a pleasant Wild West-show flavor and are excel-

"TYPE RACES" are first subdivisions of thousands of different faces available to typographer. "Ethnic groups"—labeled at right of chart—are second subdivision. No single printer has all typefaces, so editor must choose from specimen book of company that will do his typesetting.

lent for themes based on this colorful era. With many Midwest schools having centennials in this decade, we can anticipate much use for the Americans.

Ornamented letters include a wide variety; every style that does not fit neatly into some other race is lumped under this miscellaneous heading. The Ornamenteds fall into three broad subdivisions.

Any style that has something done to the face itself is called a *shaded* letter. These usually have one or more lines running through the main strokes of the letters. If any elements are added outside the face itself, the result is a *shadowed* letter. This embellishment frequently looks like a shadow cast by the letter. In the Victorian era, additions were so many and gaudy that it was sometimes difficult to see the actual letter under flowers, vines, scrolls, people, or animals that festooned it. Letters may be shaded and shadowed at the same time.

If the basic shape of the letter is drastically changed, it is called a *Novelty* face. A typical example is the Latin letters (those we use for English) drawn to resemble Japanese or Chinese characters.

Ornamented letters are like prune whip. It's mighty tasty at Christmas or for formal banquets; if we had to eat it every day we would soon grow tired of it. In the same way Ornamented letters can easily become too much of a good thing in a yearbook.

The final type category is *Written*, which has two subdivisions. As the name indicates, both resemble handwriting. *Cursive* type has unjoined letters; *Script* letters are connected. There are literally hundreds of Written faces ranging from the formal Spencerian, based on meticulous nineteenth-century handwriting, to casual Scripts that look as if they were done hastily with a paint brush. Written faces can be attractive in yearbooks but must be used sparingly. They are not quite as cloying as Ornamenteds, but danger of overuse is always present.

A variation of the Written faces is *calligraphy*, literally translated as "beautiful writing." Calligraphy is handlettering. It is highly attractive when done by an expert; unfortunately, skilled calligraphers are rare and command handsome fees.

Calligraphy's major advantage is flexibility. In regular type, every *h* looks like every other. In calligraphy, the artist changes the form slightly to make it blend more harmoniously with its neighbors. In the word *his*, for instance, the artist might make the top of the *h* swoop over and turn into the dot on the *i*.

Handlettering can, of course, be used to produce faces of any type race. But it should be used in yearbooks only if an exceptionally talented letterer is on the staff. Letter designing is a highly specialized art form; few commercial artists have mastered it. Even fewer students can letter beautiful, legible alphabets. If any flat injunction can be applied to yearbook production, it would be this: *Never use amateur handlettering!!*

There is really no need to; there are so many faces available that practically any effect can be obtained by using regular type.

Type Terminology

The staff should know some of the more widely used terms of the typographer.

We are all familiar with *capitals*: ABCD. The *small letters*—abcd—are called *lowercase* or *minuscules*. There are also *small caps*—ABCD—which have the form of capitals but the height of minuscules.

The imaginary line on which the letters stand is the *baseline;* the equally imaginary one across the top of acmnwx is the *meanline.* Any part of a letter that projects below the baseline is a *de-*

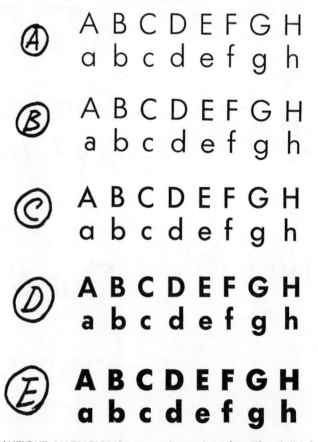

WEIGHT VARIATIONS create "series" within "family" of type. These are variations on Spartan, classical Sans Serifs ethnic of Monotonal race. A: Light; B: Book; C: Medium; D: Heavy; E: Black. There are two more weights in family; Bold, which comes right after Medium, and Extra Black, very heaviest. Using various weights of face can give pleasant variety within yearbook, while assuring typographic harmony that comes from using single family.

scender and a letter that has such a projection is also called a *descender*. For instance, this term applies to both the letter *p* and to its "tail." Extensions above the meanline are *ascenders* and that name also applies to the letter that owns such a neck, such as *b, h,* and *d.*

Three basic variations on the design of a letter are: width, weight, and angle. The normal width of a letter is rarely mentioned; we just take it for granted. If the height remains the same but the width of the letter is broadened, the result is an *Expanded* face. If the face is squeezed together, but no change made in height, it is *Condensed.* (Condensed faces are hard to read, and their use should be avoided.)

If the width and height of a letter remain constant but the thickness of the stroke is increased, it is a *Bold, Heavy,* or *Black* face. Thinning the stroke produces a *Light, Thin,* or *Book* weight.

We have already looked at letters that slant to the right; they are Italics or Obliques. Those that slant to the left are *Backslants;* they are ugly and hard to read and, fortunately, rare. No good typographer would use a Backslant in a yearbook.

Type sizes used in large masses are called *body type.* These include 5½-, 6-, 7-, 8-, 9-, 10-, 11- and 12-point. Depending on their use, 14-point faces may be body types on occasion.

Display sizes are those that are used as headlines. These include 14-, 18-, 24-, 36-, 48-, 60- and 72-point. There are also 30- and 42-point, but these are not considered part of the normal schedule. There are larger sizes (120-point is not rare), but these are not often used in yearbooks. Twelve-point may be a display size at times; the distinguishing factor is the use, not the size.

Printer's Measurement

While the staff is learning a little about type faces, it might as well learn the printer's system of measurement. He doesn't use inches; his units are the *point* and the *pica.* A point is 1/72 of an inch; a pica is 12 points. Professionals do all their layouts in these two units; the yearbook staff should do the same.

The size of type is designated in points, but this can cause some confusion. A 10-point letter, for instance, means only that the size of the metal block that supports the printing character is 10 points tall. Thus it is possible—and it does happen—that a 10-point face may actually be smaller than a 9-point one because it doesn't use up all the available space on the metal carrier.

Horizontal spacing in printing is produced by using *ledds,* strips of metal 2 points thick. The proper spelling is *leads* but the phonetic form is growing in use. A *slug* is 6-points thick and a *reglet* is 12 points (a pica), or even thicker. Spacing between lines is called *ledding;* it can be as little as a half point.

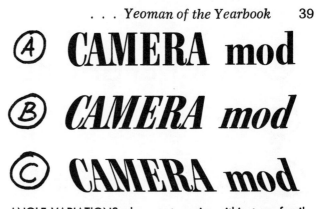

ANGLE VARIATIONS also create series within type family. A is normal vertical form called "Roman" within that race and "Perpendicular" in all other races. B is slanted to right, forming "Italic" in Roman race, "Oblique" in all others. C is "Backslant," ungainly form that finds little favor among professional typographers. (Note that all parts of name of typeface are capitalized.)

The study of type is so fascinating that the student staffer may be bitten by the bug. If he is, it's a pleasant malady, and there are many excellent and enjoyable books on the subject in most libraries.

Body Type

Body type not only is unobtrusive, it's supposed to be. Most readers of books take it for granted; they see only the words, the type is "invisible." But it is important, and its selection is the first the editor must make.

He should ask the printer for a specimen book or sheet which shows all typefaces available in that shop. There is no point in choosing an exotic face such as *Serbian No. 10,* then finding out that only two printers in all the United States have it— and his printer isn't one of them.

For body type, the editor should choose one with high *readability.* This is the characteristic that makes it easy and pleasant to read large masses of type. Romans have the highest readability, so most books (as this one) are set in Roman. Sans Serifs have low readability; do not choose a Sans for your book even though your uninitiated staff may prefer it.

Some popular, and highly readable, body faces are: Primer, Century Schoolbook, Caledonia, Fairfield, Electra, Times Roman, Corona, Baskerville, Bodoni Book, Caslon. This must be a partial list; a complete one would fill this whole page and more.

The editor must also choose the *duplex.* This is something like using the shift key on a typewriter. But instead of changing from lowercase to capitals, the duplex gives either boldface or Italic variations of the basic face. For yearbook use, the Italic is more useful in the duplex.

The size of body type is a vital contributor to good readability. Nothing smaller than 8-point should be used in a book; 10-point is much better.

WIDTH VARIATIONS shown here are all within popular Gothic family, Univers. (That's right; without an e at the end.) A: Normal width; B: Extended; C: Condensed; D: Extra Condensed. In all instances, height remains same. "Normal" series—with few exceptions—carry only family name; adjective "normal" or "regular" is understood.

Variations of any kind carry family name and one or more appropriate adjectives. Face may be varied in more than one way, so we might have "Bold Extended Oblique," for instance, showing all three possible changes.

For 8-point type, ledding of a half-point should be used between lines. For 9- through 12-point, ledding should be a full 1 point.

Most printers can show the editor specimens of body type *set solid* (with no extra space between lines) and ledded a half and a full point. This is the only way to make a choice. If you see just a single line or two of body type, you probably will see no difference between two faces; only in a sizable block do the differences become apparent. But your reader will see body type only in blocks, remember.

Copy

The word *copy* has several meanings in yearbook usage. Most commonly it means the written material that will be set in body type to create a *copy block*. Copy also means any material, except the dummy, that is sent to the printers, so copy is headline, caption, and cutline material as well as artwork used for platemaking.

Caption Type

The explanatory matter that accompanies pictures should be set in a face that is noticeably different from the body type. This matter is usually called a *caption*, but if it is just the name of a person, it is the *ident*, short for *identification*.

Common in newspapers but fairly new and rare in yearbooks are the *i&e lines*. The *i* stands for *ident* and the *e* for *expository*, a line explaining the ident. The i-line is usually set all-cap and the e-

line in lower case of the same face. The result is:

MARILYN BASKINS
. . . *winner of Alumnae Cup*

The e-line always begins with an *ellipsis*, those three little dots that indicate a link to preceding material.

Sans Serifs are excellent for this matter because they contrast so much to body type that there will be no danger of the reader inadvertently wandering from one block of type to another.

As we have noted, the Sans have low readability. But they have high *legibility*. This is the quality that makes a comparatively few words easy to absorb quickly, almost in a single glance. We use legible type for headlines, for instance. Captions are comparatively short, and here legibility is desirable. We also use Sans in those instances when there may be large masses of type but the reader is interested in only a small portion of it. This is true of idents, for instance; the reader actually looks for only one name to match up with a face. He may repeat the process over and over but at any given time he is reading only a word or two.

Eight-point makes a good size for captions and idents in most Sans Serifs faces. But there may be a wide difference in the actual size of the type although two or more faces may have the same point size. If the face you are considering is not *big on the slug*—that is, it doesn't use the full height of the metal carrier for the character—it may be necessary to use 9- or 10-point. With some faces, and if the need to save space is pressing, a 6-point Sans may be adequate. The only way to determine this exactly is to study and compare each available choice carefully.

Sans Serifs require less ledding than Romans, so ½-point extra spacing between lines of a caption is usually adequate.

Use of Body Type

Once the typeface, size, and ledding have been chosen, the staff must adopt standards for the proper use of type.

An important factor in readability of body type is the *line length* or *measure*. A type line narrower than 12 picas, or wider than 24 picas, is difficult to read. Therefore the staff should choose basic *column widths* that are well within the extremes of readability.

It will make it easier for everyone involved—staff, printer, and, most important, reader—if all typesetting is in one of three basic column widths.

For larger pages, 9 × 12 and 8½ × 11 inches, the best settings are 13 picas (which means you can get three columns on a page); 18 picas (two columns per page); and 24 picas (a single column with plenty of white space or room for pictures).

For the 7¾ × 10½-inch page, settings should be 12 picas (for a 3-column page); 18 picas (for two columns); and 24 picas.

Any other line lengths should be avoided; they contribute nothing to readability, little to attractive page layouts, and much to inefficiency and useless typesetting costs.

Above all, avoid the use of *runarounds*. This is the shortening of a series of lines within a block of copy so that a picture or portion thereof can be set into the rectangle of type.

On senior portrait pages, settings will be in different units, of course. The narrowest "line" would be the width of a single picture. If the senior directory, the listing of activities for each graduate, runs on the picture pages, it will require a second, wider line. Captions can be set in regular column measures.

Names under senior portraits are best in Sans Serifs. The senior directory may be in either Sans or Romans. If a small size—6-point—is used for identifying pictures, it is wise to use a larger size—8- or 10-point—for the directory.

In all these instances, suggestions are directed to the ideal conditions. If your printer doesn't have all the sizes suggested here, don't panic. It will not hurt your yearbook much—if any—to use alternate sizes.

In large masses of body type, *paragraph starters* may be required to relieve the dull gray area. If the block of body type is at a distance—or separated by some other element—from the headline, the graf-starter acts as a little magnet to direct the eye to the starting point of the text.

The most used is an *initial*, which may be just a larger size of the body type or headletter or a more ornate letter from the Ornamented race. Most frequently used is the headletter.

A *rising* or *stickup* initial is one that aligns with the baseline of the first line of body type and projects upward. This is the easiest for the staff and printer to handle. An *inset* or *sunken* initial is one that occupies a top left corner cut out of the rectangle of body type. Sunken initials should align precisely with the lowest line of adjacent body type and with the top of the first line of body matter. Alignment is often difficult and this is a good reason that sunken initials are used quite rarely now. Sunken initials are specified as *two-line* or *three-line* initials to show how many lines of body type must be shortened to make room.

If the initial starts a word, it is usually set in small caps. If the initial is a word in itself, the next word or two—between six and ten letters—are set small-cap. But a closely linked phrase should not be split between small caps and lowercase. If the opening phrase is *The Dramatic Club offered,* etc., and the T is an initial, either only HE or HE DRAMATIC CLUB should be in small caps

(not HE DRAMATIC club).

Other paragraph starters are stars, squares, flat triangles that resemble arrows, and a mark that looks like a reverse P with two vertical strokes appropriately called a *paragraph mark*.

In newspapers and magazines, occasional paragraphs of boldface or italics are used to break up masses of regular body type. In yearbooks the

HANDLETTERING done by amateurs should be avoided as two examples above strongly indicate.

When done by professionals—such as Raymond DaBoll who did handsome specimens below—handlettering has elegance. When in written form, it is called "calligraphy."

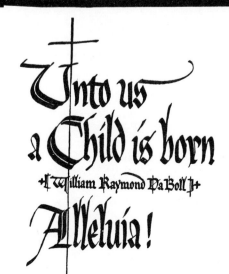

technique is not good. Large masses of boldface will create blotches on a page; large areas of Italics will scare away the reader. The average person thinks Italics is hard to read. It isn't; but his mistaken belief is sufficient to make the job distasteful.

Sans Serifs really do have low readability and should not be used in masses.

The practice of boldfacing names in a block of copy ought to be avoided. The bold names stand out like measles and their effect on reading is not pleasant; you would not enjoy it if a person speaking with you in a normal tone should shout out every proper name.

Body Typesetting Styles

Body type is most attractive on a page when it is *justified,* with both margins evenly aligned. (The type on this page is justified.) No special instructions need be given the typesetter to achieve this effect; that's the way he'll set it unless told otherwise. Copy to be set in justified lines is marked like this:

Bodoni Book 10/11—18 picas

The name, of course, indicates the typeface to be used. The first number (10) is the point size. The second number (11) is the point size of the entire line, type and interlineal spacing. In this case, 1 point of ledding will be used; this 1 point, plus the 10 points of type gives a line 11 points high. The final number tells the measure, the length of the line. Justification is done by the typesetter; he fills out each line with the necessary characters no matter how the typewritten copy carries the words. A line of typescript may make more or less than a line of type. Type name and size, ledding, and measure are basic instructions that must be given for every unit of type.

On occasion, however, the writer wants to have a line of type contain only those characters that are in a line of typewriting. In that case he will add, to the basic type instruction, the phrase:

Set line for line.

The results of such instructions might well be a block of type that looks like this:

This type
has been set
in the style the printer calls
"line for line."
The typewritten manuscript
has been written
in a form
exactly as it appears in type.

You will notice that this example aligns at the

left but not at the right. This style is called *flush left*. To instruct the printer, the copyreader would write

Set flush left

on the copy, immediately after the basic instruction. To reenforce the instruction, he would draw two vertical, parallel lines in the left margin of the typewritten copy.

The opposite style of setting is *flush right*. Instructions are the phrase, *Set flush right,* written after the basic specification, with parallel lines drawn in the right margin of the copy.

This is a sample
of type
set flush right.
Note that the left margin
is ragged.

That ragged left margin makes flush-right setting less than desirable. Each time the reading eye has finished a line, as it comes back to start the next line, it must look for the starting point. This doesn't take a lot of time, of course; the eye doesn't have to look over a 10-acre field. But it does prevent the smooth eye flow that is necessary for the most pleasant reading.

Another style of typesetting is *centered*. The result looks like this sample:

Each line
of type has been
centered
in this example.

Instructions to the printer are *Center* and a line is drawn down each margin of the copy. Little horizontal lines are drawn at each end of the longer one so it looks like a very wide, flat U lying on its side.

Each of the three latter styles is usually set line for line, and that phrase is included in instructions. If *Set line for line* is not included, the typesetter will break each line where it is mechanically most feasible. This may break closely linked phrases, a bad practice.

The question of *widow lines* as it affects copywriting has already been discussed in Chapter 2. In some instances they are also typographic problems.

Of course, there are times when a widow mars the appearance of a page. The good book designer tries to avoid a widow at the top or bottom of a column because it breaks a neat rectangle of type. In this case "widow" is usually defined as less than a half line. A widow consisting of a short word or part of a word is especially disturbing in this placement. It is even worse when a reader hits a hyphen at the end of a column, takes a long trek to the head of the next column and finds just a few letters there.

In such cases, the widow can be eliminated by adding words to the last line or by eliminating or shortening words in previous lines to effect enough space to accommodate the leftovers. Ideally, these changes should be made in the line immediately above the widow. The higher the editor goes up into the paragraph, the more resetting of type is required and the greater the expense of alterations.

Suppose, in the paragraph we have just read, the editor changes a word in the very first sentence. Instead of "eliminating" he uses "killed" in order to gain six characters. The typesetter would have to reset the entire paragraph. Not only is this costly, but it creates opportunity for more errors. Oddly enough, errors are more plentiful in such resetting than in the original setting.

Any changes that must be made in proofs to correct errors of the typesetter are made without added charges. But those changes made by the editor are called *author's alterations, AA's*. They are charged, directly or indirectly, to the yearbook. They also waste precious time.

Widows can be eliminated only in proofs. There is no way of determining, in the copy, where a short line will occur. Such corrections are costly and bothersome.

The typesetter will, as part of his job, try to prevent the very worst widows. This point should be stressed in preliminary conferences with the printer.

Widows in cutlines are most distressing to yearbook staffs. A simple and effective cure is to instruct the typesetter:

Center last line.

Set in normal, justified lines, the conclusion of a set of cutlines might look like this:

> during the annual Honors As-
> sembly in April when members
> of the society were honored by
> the Alumni.

Notice the difference in appearance when the last line is centered as in this example:

> during the annual Honors As-
> sembly in April when members
> of the society were honored by
> the Alumni.

Whenever changes are made to avoid widow lines, great care must be taken that the literary quality of the copy is not marred. This requires much greater care and skill than the original writing.

Light Extra Condensed

Light

Light Italic

Light Condensed

Light Condensed Italic

Medium Extra Condensed

Medium Extended

Medium

Medium Italic

Medium Condensed

Medium Condensed Italic

Demibold Extended

Demibold

Demibold Italic

Bold Condensed

Bold Condensed Italic

Bold Extended

Bold

Bold Italic

Extra Bold Extended

UNIVERS FAMILY—race: Monotonal; ethnic group: Gothic— has 20 series, each variation upon basic design, which in this case is "Medium." There is "Light," thinner form of Medium, and three that are heavier. There are two degrees of condensing letterform and one of angle. Note that although slanted form is here called "Italic," that term properly applies only to Roman race, and here letters should be called "Oblique."

Typographic Style

The consistency that makes for pleasant reading is assured by an editorial style that is discussed in Chapter 2. A similar typographic style must be adopted to assure pleasant physical reading. Some of the usages to be decided on are:

Paragraphing. Customarily, the start of a paragraph is marked by a 1-em indent. An *em* is the square of the point size in use at the moment. If 12-point type is being set, the paragraph indention would be 12 points.

Sometimes no indent is used; extra white space separates the paragraphs. This can be attractive, but care must be taken that this extra space is not forgotten. Should that happen when the last line of a graf is full, the result will be two paragraphs running together.

As a variation, sometimes the first paragraph is not indented but all others are.

Copy to be set without indenting is marked with two little parallel lines just to the left of the first word in a *graf* and, in the left margin, is written: *No P.* The written mark is the reverse P used in copyreading.

Whereas the length of sentences and paragraphs is basically editorial style, short paragraphs are also the concern of the typographer. The length of paragraphs, like that of sentences, must vary for pleasant reading; but a dozen lines should be the absolute maximum per graf. Often paragraphing must be done to typographical standards rather than literary ones. William Faulkner wrote paragraphs that ran for several pages. He was a genius and could get away with it; the typical yearbook editor cannot.

Titles. There are several ways of setting the names of a play, musical composition, book, poem, etc. The simplest is to capitalize the title: A Midsummer Night's Dream. Frequently used is the quote style: "A Midsummer Night's Dream." Or, titles may be set off by Italicizing: *A Midsummer Night's Dream.*

If you intend to use Italics, the printer should be told this at the time body type is first selected. If the font selected is duplexed with boldface, the result will be **A Midsummer Night's Dream.** This is not very pretty.

A style used less frequently is *caps-and-small-caps—C&SC—*which sets a title as A MIDSUMMER NIGHT'S DREAM. Again, you must ask your printer if this is available in the face you have chosen.

Accents. Some writers seek a *strong* emphasis by a typographic device. The editor must decide whether Italics or boldface will be used here. Obviously this decision will be predicated on the duplex chosen for titles. It is not practical to use Italics and boldface in the same body setting.

Writing that requires a change in typeface is weak; emphasis should come from the choice of words and their placements. (Let the author defend himself by pointing out that in this book Italics are used to identify technical terms.)

Using all-capitals for emphasis is a practice to

NOVELTY FACES can give pleasant flavor to yearbook page. But editor must resist temptation to use face with too-low legibility. Even best of Novelties are so difficult to read that they should be used only with short and familiar words.

Top line here is variation of "magnetic reading" characters used on checks. Other four faces are oldtimers from turn of century. Old typefaces are frequently resurrected for brief popularity. But only thoroughly sound type designs last forever, and no typographer can go wrong by sticking with classical letterforms.

be avoided. It is comparatively DIFFICULT to read material SET IN ALL-CAPS and the APPEARANCE of such TYPE is hardly ELEGANT. This setting should be reserved for writers who use ZOOM, POWIE, BOOM and KA-POOOOOOW, along with a lot of exclamation points.

Senior Directory. If you use a senior directory, will you set names as *William A. Brown* or *Brown, William A.?* The first style is most pleasant.

Cutlines and Idents. Several style decisions are unique to the type accompanying pictures. The most important is the way to designate position.

We read pictures as we read type, left to right and top to bottom. (The author was tempted to Italicize "top to bottom" for emphasis. But he just didn't have the courage to do so after the homily of a few paragraphs ago.) But emphasis must be made because so many yearbooks identify people improperly from bottom to top.

The top line of people should be identified first, and as Top Row. Then comes Second Row, perhaps Third Row and finally, Front Row.

The editor has a choice among: Left to Right, left to right, (left to right), (l. to r.), l. to r., or from left.

At the end of the names in one row, the editor may use a period, comma, semicolon, colon, dash . . . or nothing. He must choose one.

If only names are listed, a good style is this:

> *Top row (left to right): John Jones, Polly Brown, etc. Second row: Marion Moore, Thomas Hart, etc.*

If identifications read out of text, they can be handled like this:

> *Leading cheers at the final tournament game are (from left): Jane Dilley, Priscilla Matting, etc.*

Usually identifications that read out in this fashion are not used for pictures with many individuals. But if location by rows is required, the style might be:

> *Taking a curtain call after the Spring Revue (from left): Back row: Jimmie Kurtz, Thelma Richards, etc. Center row: Billie Meyer, Lester Bewick, etc.*

If one person dominates the picture, he may be identified first:

> *Class President Johnny Jones burns the freshman beanie in traditional ceremony assisted by (from left) Polly Berdan, Gary Salvner, etc.*

Or such cutlines may be handled as:

> *Chancellor William Tomby of State University (wearing light hat) arrives on campus for Homecoming festivities. Accompanying him are (from left) Billy Jones, Sandra Highes, Principal John Wheedon, etc.*

Note that cutlines and captions are always written in the present tense. Although the action itself took place in the past, in the photo the action is now, right before the reader's eyes.

If there are five or more people in a row, a regular paragraph indent should be used at the start of each row of identifications.

When only individual portraits are used, as on a seniors page, the whole name must run under the picture. This often requires two lines of type. If senior directory material runs on the same page as the pictures, it will give the full name of the student, of course. In this case, only the last name is required under the picture. Do not—repeat, not— use one initial with the last name. This is a European practice that is almost uncouth in America.

Here the editor with good taste uses only the last name or first and last name or two initials and last name. If there are two or more students with the same last name on a page, differentiate by using first names or two initials with the last name: *R. M. Smith*, not *R. Smith*.

Folio lines. Almost every yearbook carries *folios*, page numbers. Some also carry *running folio heads.* These may be just the name of the book. Or that name may appear on even-numbered pages and the name of the section on odd-numbered pages.

The editor must choose the style and position for these elements. On smaller books, the folios are most effective at the top outside corners of the pages. On larger books they are often placed at the bottom. If running folio heads are used, they are usually combined with the folios. On left-hand pages, they would look like this:

46 THE LEGENDA

On the opposite page, the element would be either:

THE LEGENDA 47
or
SENIORS 47

Notice that the page number goes toward the outside. The running heads, or the folios alone, can be at the outside or inside corners of pages, or centered. Your author prefers running heads at the inside, folios alone at outside, corners.

Running folio heads may be in the Italic or small caps of the body type or in the face used for idents. These are admittedly a minor element in a yearbook but demand as close attention as the more obvious ones.

In some books, the folios are enclosed in brackets: [22]. This is a fussy style; the brackets serve no useful purpose.

Another ineffective style is to run the folios at the halfway point in the outside margin of a page. When a reader is looking for a page number, this placement makes them almost undetectable.

When a picture occupies the area where the folios or running heads would normally appear, they are just eliminated. You do not need folios on every page.

In fact, some editors doubt whether folios are needed at all. Only if an index is included in the book are folios necessary to help the reader find an item.

If folio numbers are not used, page dummies must still be numbered so the printer can place pages in proper order.

As with editorial style, the important thing in typographic style is consistency. If a style is correct mechanically, grammatically and by good usage, the editor may use his own preferences in making the choice. Once made, style must be followed meticulously.

Headletters

In most yearbooks, five sizes of headlines (*head-letters*) are used. For *divider pages,* it is customary to use from 36- through 72-point.

Larger books use *subdividers;* the major section on SPORTS might be broken down into FOOTBALL, TRACK, BASKETBALL, etc. These pages would use 24-, 30- or 36-point, depending on the size used for dividers.

The *main headline* on a two-page spread would be in 18- or 24-point, and *subheads* on such a page, 12- through 18-point.

If *running heads* (which we'll discuss in just a moment) are used, they will require a fifth face.

For the first four heads (or as many of them as are required for your book), it is best to stay within one *family* of type. A family is a subdivision of a race and has a family name; in the list of types given in this chapter, family names are used. Staying within one family assures pleasant typographic harmony.

For running heads, a contrasting face is most effective. This might be only a slight contrast, using an Italic with the rest of the heads in Roman. A good Script or Cursive gives more contrast and works well for running heads.

Running heads are portions of continuous copy. (They should not be confused with "running folio heads.") If the reader of a yearbook were to read only the running heads from page to page, he

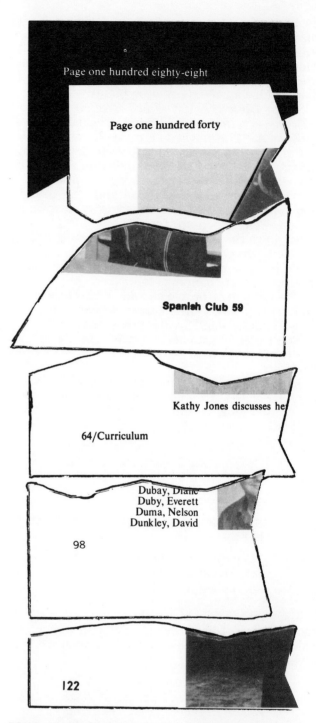

FOLIO LINES should be kept simple. Spelling out page numerals (top two examples) is less useful for reader than using only actual numbers (lower two specimens). Third example includes section heading with page number; nice touch, but probably not worth bother and expense.

would have a continuous, integrated communication as he went from beginning to back of the book. Yet on each spread the running head would be sufficiently self-contained to make sense when read alone.

Here would be a typical group of running heads in a senior portrait section, giving pleasant continuity and tying the pages together into a coherent unit:

As the Class of 1980 approaches commencement . . .
. . . it can look back on three exciting years . . .
. . . Members began their high school career in an antique building . . .
. . . but as juniors they moved into our handsome new home . . .
. . . In a $3.7 million building, called the country's most beautiful . . .
. . . our seniors began traditions that will be cherished in the future . . .

Each phrase appears on a separate spread. The use of the *ellipsis* (the three periods . . .) indicates that the copy reads from preceding phrases and into following ones.

Literary quality of running heads must be as high as possible because they are so conspicuous.

The *running* technique can be used to tie together related pictures or those in sequence. Here is typical use with a series of continuous-action sports pictures:

Terrance leaps high for a Gallagher-thrown pass . . .
. . . shakes off a West High defender . . .
. . . and crosses the chalk line for six big points.

Even if the action doesn't move from one picture to another, the *running caption* is useful:

In the busy chemistry lab . . .
. . . picturesque equipment makes a fascinating background . . .
. . . as modern alchemists mix their potions . . .
. . . and try to forget that dishes must be washed before the bell rings.

Choosing the Headletter

The choice of headline type is determined by several factors.

A good headletter must have high legibility. This rules out condensed faces such as Onyx or Campanile and eccentric Novelties or over-ornate Ornamenteds.

The headletter must have a pleasant *typographic color*. If it is too light it may be lost among dark photographs; if too dark, it may stick out like the proverbial sore thumb.

The headletter must be available in the necessary sizes so that the editor doesn't have to mix families to fill his needs.

The *accent* face—that used for running heads —should have high contrast to the regular headlines.

After those mechanical requirements have been met, the headletter should be appropriate to the theme and style of the book. Just what makes a face appropriate cannot be described in exact terms; the staff must "just feel that it's right." Peronal preferences are an entirely valid basis for a choice after technical requirements have been met.

Personality of Type

Headline type is a major factor in creating a personality for a yearbook.

Oldstyle Roman has connotations of dignity, antiquity, authority—yet, all the while, it is comfortable and almost cozy.

Modern Romans are crisp, clean and contemporary.

Text, as already noted, is the face of pomp, dignity, ceremony and religious overtones.

Sans Serifs are strong, informal and modern. Gothics are husky—almost musclebound—and very matter-of-fact. Square Serifs are sturdy, unimaginative, and neither exciting nor aesthetically pleasing.

Ornamenteds are so many it is impossible to make any blanket statement about the race other than the admonition already given: Use them as sparingly as a cook uses cayenne pepper.

The Written faces, too, come in so many varieties that they can be used all the way from formal wedding invitations to cartoon strips. Usually their legibility is low and for yearbooks they should be used as sparingly as the Ornamenteds.

The most useful and/or popular of the various races are:

Oldstyle Romans: Goudy, Century, Cheltenham Light, Caslon, Garamond (or Garamont), Times Roman.

Modern Romans (including some known technically as *Transitionals*): Bodoni, in various weights; Onyx; Campanile; Electra; Caledonia.

Text: Old English, Goudy Text, Cloister Black, American Text.

Sans Serif: Spartan, Tempo, Futura, Twentieth Century, Venus, Vogue.

Gothics: Trade Gothic, News Gothic, Franklin, Engravers, Metro, Univers, Erbar.

Square Serifs: Memphis, Cairo, Stymie, Karnak, Playbill, P. T. Barnum.

Ornamented: Narciss, Broadway, Beton, Normandia, Outline, Umbra.

Written: Kaufman Script, Cartoon, Mandate, Brush, Coronet, Hauser Script, Lydian Cursive.

This list shows less than 1 percent of the typefaces available today. Every printer will not have every one of these; he may not even have any. But he will have a functional equivalent.

Headline Style

Because headlines are so conspicuous, any mishandling is highly annoying to the reader. He may not know exactly what there is about a headline that he doesn't like; but subconsciously he realizes that something is not quite right. This irritation detracts from his pleasure in your book.

Adopt a basic headline style that is attractive and legible. There are several the editor can choose from.

All-capital setting has two advantages. Caps carry more weight than lowercase and so an all-cap head can be smaller than one in another style and still carry a page or spread. All-cap setting creates a neat band because there are no ascenders or descenders to make an irregular outline.

Such regularity, however, is a liability as far as reading is concerned. We recognize a word by its silhouette. If it is just a rectangle that all-caps create, we must then inspect the word more closely, almost letter by letter, in order to read it.

ALL-CAP SETTING LOWERS THE READABILITY OF BODY TYPE, TOO, AS THIS SHORT PARAGRAPH DEMONSTRATES. THIS DISABILITY IS NOT AS OBVIOUS IN A HEADLINE WITH ONLY A FEW WORDS. A SINGLE WORD IN CAPS IS NOT DIFFICULT TO READ.

If the editor is tempted to use all-caps, it should be for only a word or two and preferably short ones. He should carefully letter the head to see if there are combinations that will tend to fracture the word. If there are, all-caps should be avoided.

It is a good rule of thumb that Italics should never be used in all-cap setting. It is a law as immutable as that of the Medes and Persians that Text, Script, Cursive, or Ornamented letters can never be used in all-caps. They just can't be read, and there are no exceptions.

Editors should beware the temptation to swing too far from all-cap setting and use no capitals at all. It is just as much an error to spell the month "september" with a little *s*, as "zeptember" with a wrong letter.

Capitals are the signal, in English, that tells the reader that the word is a proper noun. To make *the* "John Carpenter" into *a* "john carpenter" turns an individual into a constructor of outdoor plumbing. It is a denigration he is entitled to resent. So is any person who is thus de-proper-nouned in your yearbook.

TYPOGRAPHIC DON'TS in body-type usage are shown on opposite page:

A. This line is set far too long. The black arrow indicates "optimum line length" and MX shows longest line that can be read with comfort and efficiency. MN indicates shortest line. These dimensions will vary according to lowercase-alphabet length of specific font.

B. Body type set vertically is virtually illegible as well as being far more expensive to set than in correct horizontal style.

C. When boldface is used to start paragraph, complete phrase—in this case, name of person—should be in bold. Never should closely-knit phrases be broken into two kinds of typefaces.

D. When lines are set ragged—"freefall" is technical term—they should never be hyphenated as white arrow points out here.

E. These lines are too short and thus difficult to read.

F. "Reversed type" is always hard to read. This handicap is aggravated when small type—as here, 5½ point—is used. Ten-point is smallest for reverses.

G. This is a "runaround"; the line is shortened to create an opening into which art or other type is inset. Change in reading rhythm annoys readers.

If a person is famous enough, he may choose to become an "e.e. cummings." But we must recognize this as a *nom de plume,* which is not appropriate for the typical student or teacher.

The typographer has the right to choose between all-cap or upper-and-lower setting: Both these styles are acceptable in English and are exclusively a typographic concern. But to de-capitalize a word is tampering in an area of our language in which the editor has no more prerogatives than he has to rewrite any other rules of grammar.

The most widely used headline style is called *upper-and-lower,* in which each word is capitalized.

This Is A Sample Of Upper-And-Lower Setting. It Is Easier To Read Than All-Caps But Is Not The Easiest Style For The Reader.

If the editor chooses this style, he must determine what words, if any, are not to be capped. Some publications do not cap prepositions, articles, or conjunctions unless they are the first word in the head. The word *to* is capped when used in an infinitive: *To Run;* not, *to Run.*

The major advantage of *u & lc* heads is that these are most widely used by newspapers, and this style, in itself, says "headline."

Easiest to read are *downstyle* heads. Here just the first word of a head and proper nouns are capitalized. This follows the style used in setting body type; because we read so much body type, we are most familiar with downstyle and read it with the least effort.

The editor should note that when a downstyle

MN   MX

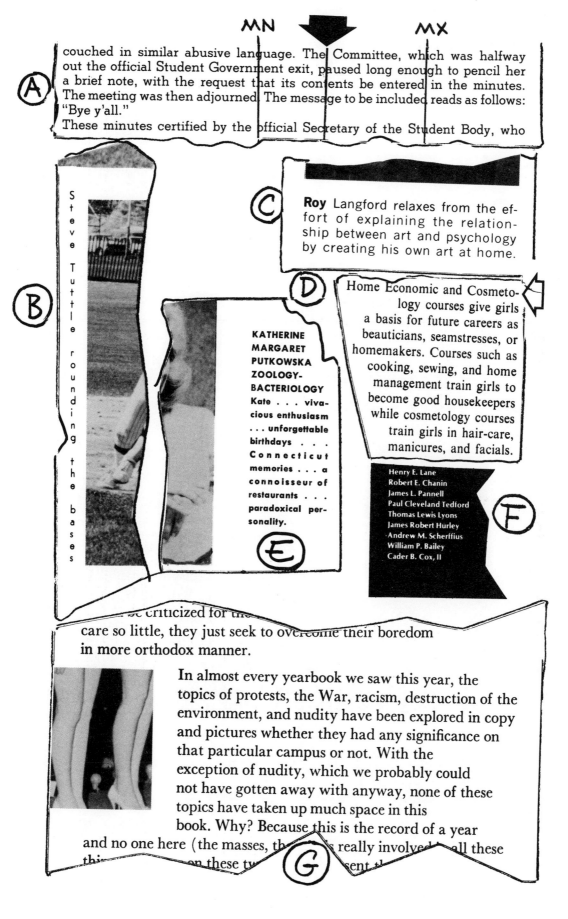

(A) couched in similar abusive language. The Committee, which was halfway out the official Student Government exit, paused long enough to pencil her a brief note, with the request that its contents be entered in the minutes. The meeting was then adjourned. The message to be included reads as follows: "Bye y'all."
These minutes certified by the official Secretary of the Student Body, who

(B) Steve Tuttle rounding the bases

(C) **Roy** Langford relaxes from the effort of explaining the relationship between art and psychology by creating his own art at home.

(D)

(E) KATHERINE MARGARET PUTKOWSKA ZOOLOGY-BACTERIOLOGY Kate . . . vivacious enthusiasm . . . unforgettable birthdays . . . Connecticut memories . . . a connoisseur of restaurants . . . paradoxical personality.

Home Economic and Cosmetology courses give girls a basis for future careers as beauticians, seamstresses, or homemakers. Courses such as cooking, sewing, and home management train girls to become good housekeepers while cosmetology courses train girls in hair-care, manicures, and facials.

(F) Henry E. Lane
Robert E. Chanin
James L. Pannell
Paul Cleveland Tedford
Thomas Lewis Lyons
James Robert Hurley
Andrew M. Scherffius
William P. Bailey
Cader B. Cox, II

be criticized for the
care so little, they just seek to overcome their boredom in more orthodox manner.

In almost every yearbook we saw this year, the topics of protests, the War, racism, destruction of the environment, and nudity have been explored in copy and pictures whether they had any significance on that particular campus or not. With the exception of nudity, which we probably could not have gotten away with anyway, none of these topics have taken up much space in this book. Why? Because this is the record of a year and no one here (the masses, the ones really involved) all these

(G)

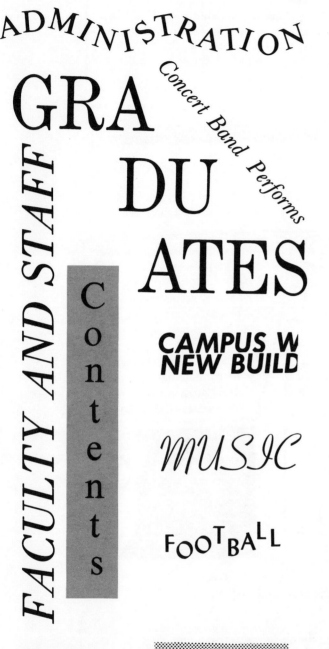

ADMINISTRATION

GRA DU ATES

Concert Band Performs

FACULTY AND STAFF

Contents

CAMPUS W
NEW BUILD

MUSIC

FOOTBALL

TABLE OF CONTENTS

TYPOGRAPHIC DON'TS include these common ones: Type running sideways (*Faculty*), vertically (*Contents*), or diagonally (*Concert Band*). Type set in wavy lines (*Administration*) or "bounced" or "jumbled" (*Football*). Type running across two or more different backgrounds (*Table of Contents*). "Stacked" type (*Campus* and *New*) and all-caps in Script, Cursive, or Text (*Music*) are difficult and sometimes impossible to read. Breaking words without hyphenation (*Graduates*) is grammatically as well as typographically appalling.

headline is set in two or more lines, only the first word in the head, not the first word of each line, is capped.

Thirty-two characters and spaces should be a maximum in one line of a head. Forty-two should be the maximum in the entire head if it is in more than one line. Nobody will be sent to jail if he uses thirty-three characters per line; but the numerical limitation is a good one to remind us that brevity is always a virtue, but especially so in headlines.

Flush-left heads are the most effective. Centered heads can be functional for some layouts. Flush-right heads should be avoided.

If a head must be set in two or more lines, great care must be taken that closely linked phrases do not break from one line to the next. We read heads line for line, rather than in the flowing continuation of body type. This headline is poor:

Jones Named Senior
Class President

The phrase "Senior Class" is, in effect, a single word and shouldn't be split. Prepositional phrases obviously must stay on one line.

All type should be set in horizontal lines. Avoid the temptation to set heads at an angle, on a curve, or running sideways.

Do not set type vertically. Orientals run their type in vertical rows and, apparently, read it that way. Occidentals cannot.

Do not break words in a headline. This admonition goes double for the abominable practice of breaking words without a hyphen.

Headlines should never be set with extra space between letters except, of course, when that is required as optical letterspacing of all caps. Condensed headletters should under no circumstances be letterspaced.

No extra space should be placed between lines of headletters. The shoulders built into the type provide all the interlineal spacing that is needed. Any more causes the heads to fall apart.

Copyfitting

As we have already noted, many problems of the typographer are also those of the writer or editor. Copyfitting, writing copy so that it fits a specific area, is one of these. This has been discussed in Chapter 2.

No matter which of the methods is used for copyfitting, the designer of the book should prepare a chart of specifications that will look something like this:

CHARACTERS PER LINE				
TYPE	*10-pica column*	*13-pica column*	*18-pica column*	*24-pica column*
10-pt. Caledonia		33	46	61
6-pt. Spartan Medium	36			
10-pt. Spartan Medium		36	51	68

You will notice that this chart shows the regular body type, Caledonia, in the three measures in which it will be set. The 6-point Spartan will be used for the senior directory, which is set in a narrower column, and the 10-point Spartan is used for captions.

When the writer is given an assignment, he is told the width at which to set his typewriter. He will then type normally, filling each line as closely as possible without hyphenating. Short lines will average out with those that exceed the set length.

It doesn't matter whether the typewriter he uses has the normal-size face, *elite,* or the larger, *pica;* the determining factor is the number of characters. But if the line length is established by linear measurement by a line printed or mimeographed on the copy paper, then the same typewriter face must be used by every writer on the staff.

The number of lines is determined by measuring the desired depth on a sample of the type—ledded the same amount as your type will be—and counting the lines.

There are other more complicated and more exact methods of determining exactly how many characters should be written to fill a given area. But the simple steps outlined here are adequate for most yearbook requirements. Variations in the area filled by set type will be slight, and necessary adjustments can be made without too much trouble.

Writing headlines to fit available space can be done by two methods. One is the process used by headline writers on newspapers who use the *unit count* system. Most lowercase letters count as 1; *m* and *w* count 1½; *i* and *l* and punctuation marks count ½. Space between words counts 1. Capitals count twice as much as their lowercase. So *M* and *W* count 3; *l* counts ½, but *L*, along with the rest of the cap alphabet, counts 2.

In some faces the *f* and *t* and *j* are so narrow they count ½. Some staffs adopt a memory device that: "*Flitjays* count a half; *wammies* count two."

By counting off sample headlines, a maximum unit count is established for each column width. The head writer then makes sure that his headlines do not exceed the maximum; danger of

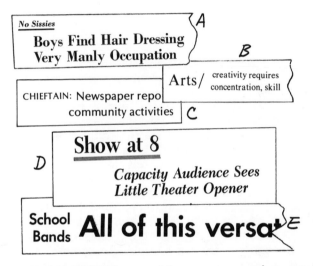

HEADLINE STYLES borrowed from newspapers have much utility for yearbooks, too.

A. "Kicker" (*No Sissies*) should be half point-size of main head. This should be written short, ideally no more than one third overall width. Main head must be indented 10 percent of overall width.

B. "Tripod" is twice size of main head. It should be about quarter length of total headline. Slash used here between tripod and main head is pleasant but unnecessary. It is too light; it ought to be thickness of *1.*

C. "Read-in." Lines of main head should align at left; so *Newspaper* and *community* should be on same left margin.

D. "Hammer," also called "reverse kicker" (*Show at 8*) should be twice point-size of main head and no wider than half of overall head length. Main head must be indented 20 percent of total width of head.

E. "Wicket" (*School Bands*) is one of few heads written flush right. It should be no more than a third of overall width of headline.

In all instances, both elements of head are in same type family, varying only in size and/or angle.

heads running too short is slight, though the head should never be shorter than 80 percent of the possible maximum.

A headline chart can be prepared that will look something like this:

| | HEADLINE CHART | | |
| | UNIT COUNT | | |
FACE	1 column (13 pica)	2 columns (27½ pica)	3 columns (42 pica)
36 Times Roman	8	18½	27½
24 Times Roman	16½	31½	57½
18 Times Roman	20½	42½	65
24 Kaufman Script	19½	41	63

Note two things about this chart: (a). Two-column heads have more characters than two one-columners because of the white space of 18 points between columns. (b). This chart should not be taken as gospel; the staff should prepare its own, using the type its own printer has. Several type companies may make the same face, yet, because of slight design differences, the unit count may vary enough to create problems if the wrong sample is used for counting.

It is wise to write heads a unit or two narrow (or to build that cushion into the counting chart). There is no danger in a short headline. But one that is too long just can't be squeezed together; type—as any printer will tell you—is made of metal, not rubber.

In many yearbooks, headlines are not written in column widths; they must be fitted in between pictures and/or copy blocks and so their length varies constantly. The maximum characters must be precounted, from a sample, for almost every head.

Suppose a headline must be written in 24-point Times Roman and the line must be 22 picas long. The head writer looks up this type in the specimen type book or sheet that must be in the office of every yearbook. He measures 22 picas on a specimen line and counts the allowable units.

A method that works most of the time is to measure off the required line length on the sample and type it on a piece of copy paper. Specimen lines are often phrases, and the 22-pica line might come out like this:

The Selection of Type Sty
Immediately under this line, the writer types his first try at the headline:

The Selection of Type Sty
Debaters sweep state tournament

Obviously that is too long. So he tries again:

The Selection of Type Sty
Debaters sweep state contest
Debaters are state champs

The last one ought to fit. For a quick check the writer counts two *t*'s in the sample line and three in the head; he has gained a half-unit. There are no *m*'s or *w*'s in the sample; there is one *m* in the head. The extra half-unit required for the *m* is offset by that gained by the third *t*. If there is any doubt, the writer can count both lines by units.

The size of the headline should be in proportion to the page. There is often a tendency to use too-large type. Sometimes the editor wants to use large type but recognizes that this makes a concentration of ink that is too heavy for his layout. So he *screens down* the type. This is done by having the platemaker, by means of the *Ben Day process*, place a pattern of tiny white dots evenly over the entire type area. The effect is that of gray type.

Screening is frowned upon by most typographers. The tiny dots produce a ragged edge along the edges of the character and, on those faces that have very thin strokes, the dot may even sever such a line.

If a headline and subhead appear on the same spread, there should be a size difference of two steps. A 36-point headline should have nothing larger than 18-point as a subhead; from 24-point, the subhead should be stepped down to 14-point.

A periodic trend is to run type *in reverse*, so it looks like white type on a black or colored background. This may be satisfactory for a very few words under very specific conditions. But it makes for difficult reading of body type in large masses.

That is because, on a sheet of printing, we "see" the dominant image first. In this case that dominant image is the black background. After we have "seen" it and attempted to "read" it, we realize that this is not the image we seek. We have to look deliberately for the weaker, negative image and "read" it. This is an annoying and inefficient process.

If type must be reversed, nothing smaller than 10-point ought to be used. Modern Romans, or any face with thin lines, should be avoided. If there is too much ink on the press—a common danger when running large reverses—the excess is forced into the white "holes" in the plate and the thin

ORGANIZATIONS

DECORATIVE BORDER

BEAUTIES

Janet Post
Tom Spencer

Friends

Mayor-for-a-Day

Bill Rainey—Mayor

Heads City Council

Practical experience in citizenship and civic affairs was the purpose of the sixteenth an-
Mayor f   a-Day project h

TYPOGRAPHIC DON'TS include these unusually bad practices: Type so poorly designed that we don't know whether
it was misspelled "Organizacions" or if that fifth-last character is actually a *T*. (It is, in this odd face!)

Text letters (as in the second line) are illegible in all-cap.
So are letters set so closely that they overlap (*Beauties*) or
when type runs across a variegated or competing background (*Janet Post* and *Friends*).

Body type, especially, cannot be read on a mottled background (lower right). In the head (*Bill Rainey*) there is too
much "ledding," spacing between lines. There should be no
such extra spacing in any headlines.

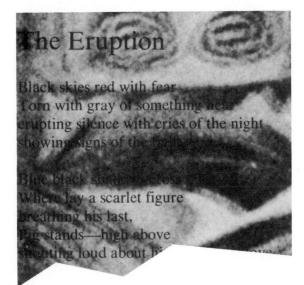

The Eruption

Black skies red with fear
Torn with gray of something
erupting silence with cries of the night
showing signs of the

Blue black
Where lay a scarlet figure
breathing his last,
Pig stands—high above
shouting loud about

TYPOGRAPHIC DON'T: Body type run over a mottled background has very low (or even no) legibility. This specimen
is same size as it appeared in yearbook.

lines are plugged up. This reduces legibility still further.

Type—be it black or white—can be read only after it has been seen. To be seen requires a maximum contrast between type and the background. Therefore a gray background, for either black or white type, reduces the contrast and lowers legibility and readability.

When type runs on a colored background, in either positive or reverse, it must be determined beforehand that the tonal values of the two elements are in adequate contrast. Red has heavy tonal value. (If you take a black-and-white picture of a red flower, it will look black. And that's the way tonal value is determined: How dark would this color appear in a b&w picture?) Thus black, with the deepest tonal value, is most difficult to read against a red background. White on yellow is just as bad on the other end of the scale.

All suggestions in this chapter are rules of thumb. Skilled typographers can, and do, break rules with happy results. The beginning typographer, however, will have best results if he follows them zealously.

There is one basic principle that can never be breached with impunity:

Type was made to be read.

The function of type is to convey information, not be part of an abstract design. Whenever the editor faces a decision on the use of type, he should ask himself a simple question: Will this usage make it easier, more convenient or more pleasant for the reader? If the answer is *Yes*, the technique is correct.

The embryo typographer needs no other guideline than a constant desire to serve the reader best.

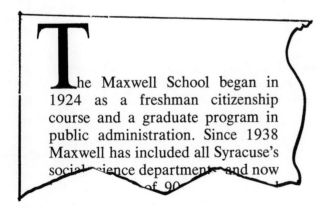

Amid whispers of, "Hush, be quiet," Miss Spooner and Miss Lamb regulated library activities. Some students studied, read, and

Seniors searched for imaginative ideas for their many compositions. Seniors, braving Advanced English, found themselve

Large balloons carried by students went bobbing down the school's halls. Unsuspecting teachers jumped

With the new math section in full swing, students hurried to class to complete unfinished assignments or brief notes before the study bell

During the opening weeks of school, frantic students pleaded with guidance counselors for last minute schedule changes, but they soon discovered revised of

INITIALS always create more problems than they solve. From the top down: *A* is too far away from rest of letters in word and so reads like two words. *S* is also too far away, and *L*, because of the large area of white its two lines enclose, seems even farther from its word. *L* properly aligns with bottom of second line of body type; but it should not project above top line.

W aligns properly at top but, of course, not at bottom. It joins properly with *ith* but—alas!—initial is crooked. *D* extends into margin. All examples are "inset" or "sunken" initials.

RISING INITIAL, *T*, is properly aligned with bottom of first line of body type. It lines up at margin with mass of letter and so left arm properly extends into margin.

This initial is easiest for printer to handle. And, as it rises above its paragraph, it builds in area of white space at its right.

Customarily, when decorative initial is used, rest of word it forms is set in "small caps." Such letters are in form of regular capitals but are of same height as primary lowercase characters.

Pictures

4

... Mirrors of School Life

Some primitive people refuse to pose for a photographer because they fear that he will capture part of their soul in the photographic image. There is a logic in that attitude, since a good photo does capture far more of a person than the reflection of light off his face and body.

The yearbook staff should always seek those photos that capture the spirit. Ideally, the reader should not say, "That is a picture of John and Mary," but "That is John and Mary."

In most yearbooks, photography is a combination of work by student and professional cameramen. Ratios vary, and the staff must divide the work according to available talent and facilities.

Individual and large group portraits are best assigned to the pro. The mass of labor involved is usually more than the student photographer can do with justice to his school work; large group portraits require experience and skill that few students have had a chance to acquire.

But there is opportunity and need for student cameramen. They are on the scene to shoot unexpected events; they blend into the surroundings so they can take candid shots without the subjects' becoming self-conscious. They know their subjects well.

Darkroom Procedures

The student photographer needs adequate equipment and working space, though neither need be elaborate. (There are so many good books available on the subject that this one need not explore the subject.) Most staffs find that *reflex*

cameras are best suited to their work. Although small 35-millimeter cameras are popular, those that use larger film have the advantage of minimizing grain or defects when extreme enlargement is required.

(In order to keep a large image on the film, cameramen should be encouuraged to move in on their subjects, to use the whole negative for the desired image.)

In the darkroom, the photographer should stick to chemicals and procedures recommended by the maker of the film he uses. Uniform processing will produce the best pictures, and in case something goes wrong, it is easier to find just where the trouble lies. There should be no improvisation of "recipes" in the darkroom.

Nor should the cameramen change from one brand to another of photographic supplies. All the standard brands are of excellent quality; but once a decision has been made on film, paper, and chemicals, the staff should use only those. This will standardize production for greater efficiency and economy.

The darkroom must be kept off-limits to everyone but staff photographers. At the end of each day, the room must be carefully housecleaned. A dirty, disorderly darkroom cannot be tolerated. Its offense to the esthetic senses can be overlooked, but contamination of chemicals and dust on negatives and enlargers result in diaster of magnitude.

Films should be processed without delay. This spreads a big job over consistent and shorter periods. The layout job doesn't become bottlenecked. When a shot is spoiled—and that happens even to the best of the pros—the error is found in time to correct it.

If there are no facilities available in the school, there are usually a few students who have some kind of darkroom in their homes.

Many staffs work out arrangements with their professional photographer to use his facilities for some of their work. The pro may do all the developing while the student does the enlarging. The pro may allow the student to use his darkroom at certain times of the day or week. In this case the student must be especially neat and careful and, obviously, must act like any well-mannered guest.

Deadlines are as important for the photo staff as for any others working on a yearbook. Little editorial work can be done until photos are ready, and deadlines must be established to give sufficient lead time for copy and layout people to meet their printer's deadlines.

Photo Assignments

Photo assignments must be made well in advance. Editors can draw up at least a tentative schedule during the summer, or even in spring. This should be made firm as soon as possible.

The simplest method for controlling photo pro-

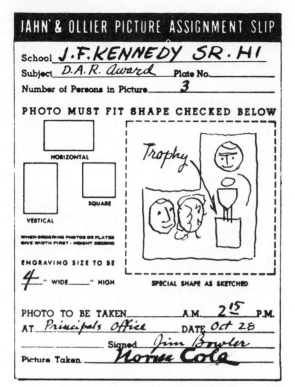

JAHN' & OLLIER PICTURE ASSIGNMENT SLIP

School _J.F. KENNEDY SR. HI_
Subject _D.A.R. Award_   Plate No. _____
Number of Persons in Picture _____3_____

PHOTO MUST FIT SHAPE CHECKED BELOW

HORIZONTAL

VERTICAL   SQUARE

WHEN ORDERING PHOTOS OR PLATES
GIVE WIDTH FIRST· HEIGHT SECOND

Trophy

SPECIAL SHAPE AS SKETCHED

ENGRAVING SIZE TO BE
_4_ " WIDE _____ " HIGH

PHOTO TO BE TAKEN _____ A.M. _2¹⁵_ P.M.
AT _Principals Office_   DATE _Oct 28_
_____   Signed _Jim Bowler_
Picture Taken _Norm Cole_

PHOTO ASSIGNMENT CARD should give all information cameraman needs. Some cards give extra points: Whom to contact, what props to take along, what extra lighting may be required. If unusual shape of picture is needed for layout (as here), rough sketch will help create proper grouping. In many cases, editor asks photographer to write left-to-rights on back of this card.

duction is a chart that shows, in columns: Assignment, initials of the assigned cameraman, deadlines for arranging pictures that require appointments, making the shot, processing film, delivering contact prints, and delivering final glossies. If different people are involved, an immediately adjacent column shows their initials. A final column indicates needed reshooting. In that case the assignment is rewritten lower on the sheet.

As each step is completed, the appropriate area is circled, blue for on-times, red for late ones.

With this method, the editor must brief the photographer on specific requirements. Such briefing should be done in all instances although the second method of assignment carries much of the instructions on *assignment slips*.

The slip shows the assignment, number of people to be in the picture, date, time, and place. It also shows the shape desired. It is signed by the editor of the section involved—so that the cameraman can easily find him for preshooting consultation. If the photo staff has several members, the one to take the picture may also be indicated. This enables using special talents; the one who is particularly able on sports shots will usually do better on such assignments than he might on a group portrait.

Often, of course, assignments must be given to the cameraman who is available at the right time.

The slips are made out with carbon copies. This precludes losing a slip—and a picture.

Both slips are stored in a series of flat, open

NOTICE OF PHOTO APPOINTMENT is given to organization or individual by form like this. It includes phone number to call if appointment must be changed, tells what clothes to wear, and/or what props to bring.

NOTICE OF Photo Appointment

Date: _1-12-73_
To: _Future Teachers_
    (NAME OF GROUP)
Attn. _Beverly Santori c/o Miss Mantell_
    (NAME OF INDIVIDUAL)

Your group has been scheduled to be photographed for the (date and name of yearbook) at the following time and place

Place: _Physics Lab_
Room Number (if any) _# 117_
Time _3:10 pm Wed. Jan. 19_
Photographer assigned _David Revett_
    (NAME)
Copywriter assigned _Sue Darcy_
    (NAME)
Charge to your organization $ _none_
Special instructions: _Each person bring at least five books_

Unless we hear differently we will assume that you will keep this appointment. If not able to do so, call (telephone number here) and advise
    by _Matthew Loomis_
    NAME OF PERSON
    DATE _Extension 317_
    Home 446-2599

boxes or on hooks. Nine spaces are required. They are labeled for each day of the week with an extra for NEXT WEEK and another for FUTURE, longer than a week in advance. Some staffs like a tenth box or hook, ANYTIME, to be done at the cameraman's convenience.

As soon as a slip is made out, it and the carbon are placed in the FUTURE file. Eight days before the assignment is to be shot, it goes into the NEXT WEEK file. Each day, as a hook is cleared of its assignments, it is refilled with those for that day of next week. The moving up is done the last thing every day, just before the editors close shop.

The cameraman going on assignment takes the slip with him; he uses the back to write identifications. (It is the responsibility of the photographer to get the idents. If a writer is assigned, too, it may be more convenient for him to make identifications, especially with large groups. But the cameraman is responsible and must check that this essential task has been done.) The carbon of the assignment slip goes to the desk of the assigning editor as the cameraman is leaving.

When the shot has been made, the original slip goes to the editor, who matches it to the carbon. Any unpaired carbons are a signal of a snafu and the editor follows up right away.

All assignments must be filled. It is rank discourtesy to stand up a subject; it usually inconveniences many staffers who are awaiting the photo to start layouts. If the cameraman cannot take an assignment, he should notify the assigning editor immediately so that a pinch-hitter can be sent or the picture rescheduled.

Even with this slip system, a preshooting conference makes sure that the cameraman knows exactly what is required, what equipment will be required, and any unusual aspects or difficulties that might be anticipated.

Student Portraits

Portraits—especially those of seniors—are certainly among the most important elements in a

good yearbook. "This is a good yearbook" is most frequently translated into "I liked my picture in the book."

Because pages of portraits occupy such a large portion of the book, they have a major effect on deadlines. As editors set deadlines for the photographer, they must remember to include time for actual shooting, developing and contact printing, selection of the portraits to be used, final printing, plus, of course, laying out the pages. There must be some insurance time, too; things do go wrong. The staff must discuss these needs in detail with the photographer. Once the deadlines have been set, they must be observed as if they were acts of Congress.

Two weeks before shooting begins, an instruction sheet should be sent to all students who will have individual portraits made. This should be carefully written to emphasize that its object is to make everyone happy, not to impose the taste of the staff upon the student body. Sugarcoated for diplomacy, the instructions will tell the student:

1. *Wear simple and appropriate clothing.* Boys will look best in necktie and jacket with solid, light-colored shirts. (Some boys don't own jackets; the staff should arrange to have a couple available at the studio.) Girls should wear simple blouses or sweaters; conspicuous fabric patterns are exaggerated in photos. Dark hair looks best with light clothing; blondes may wear dark garments.

Sorority drapes, fabric fashioned in a deep V off the outside of the shoulders, should be avoided. Rarely does this extreme style flatter the subject. Such draping is usually an intermittent fad; the

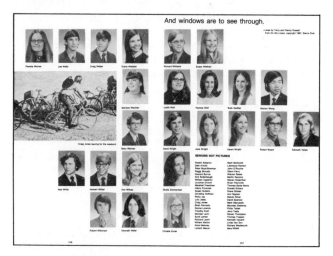

SENIOR PORTRAITS are best presented in varying page patterns. Head sizes should always be identical. White space should be kept at outside of grouping (as here). At lower right of spread above, is list of "seniors not pictured." This is not felicitous phrase; much better would be "other graduating seniors." Also to be tabooed is "not in picture" or similar phrases. This applies to any group picture as well as those groupings of individual ones.

CHECKERBOARD PATTERNS, created by ganging senior portraits in completely filled blocks, may be remedied by these techniques. In top row, school seal replaces one picture. Middle row, one portrait is silhouetted, and, bottom row, one picture is modified by snipping corners. There are other variations of changing rectangular photo to other geometric form. Always shape should be kept simple.

steven budney   joann buettner   donna buiso   marilyn buzolich   robin bundow

CHECKERBOARD PATTERN is broken by moving one name from below portrait to above it. (Unfortunately in this example, names are misspelled with small letters instead of capitals that proper nouns require.)

Only one style of variation should be used throughout section, and technique should be used sparingly, not more than once in any block of pictures.

staff should flatly refuse to be stampeded into accepting this whim. The question should not be decided by class elections; the staff, familiar with the needs of the yearbook, must make the decision—even if it is momentarily unpopular.

2. *Prepare your hair.* Boys should get a haircut about a week before; girls should have permanents, shampoos, and sets about four days in advance.

Hair styling should be simple. Girls should avoid elaborate hairdos. Coiffures, male and female, are subject to the vagaries of fashion; the more striking the style, the shorter its life. If you need arguments to bolster this, look at a yearbook of twenty years ago. Notice that those people with simple hair styles look attractive; those who were atop the wave of fashion at that moment look odd today.

3. *Go easy on jewelry.* Anything more flashy than a simple strand of pearls will make a girl look like the temptress in a late, late movie; large earrings, bracelets, and necklaces should be avoided like bubonic bacteria. Boys should check their lapel pins; photography exaggerates such jewelry to the size of a traffic cop's badge.

4. *Go easy on makeup.* Only light face powder and lipstick are necessary—and most students look their best without even that. By all means leave off eye makeup; unless it is applied by a professional, it will make a girl look like the last reel of a horror movie.

The photographer, too, should have detailed instructions. Better put it in writing that he must:

1. *Avoid theatrical poses.* Full-face or three-quarter poses are the best. Profiles and semiprofiles don't wear well; and they certainly create problems when they must be placed looking off the edge of a page!

"Glamour poses," which put the body in an unnatural position or tilt the head at an acute angle, soon look like the display cases of a theater showing old movies.

Some students may insist on Hollywood poses; *de gustibus non est disputandum.* The photographer may have to make such portraits, as the student is a customer. But the staff is not obliged to use such a picture. So at least one picture must be made to the staff's specifications, and the student should be informed that only this shot will be used in the yearbook.

2. *Use the same background and lighting for all portraits.* There must be some variations, of

PORTRAIT VARIATIONS should never create head size larger than others (as that indicated by arrow). Picture above arrowed one has too much space at right of head, and one to right of that has excess space at its left. Portrait at right of arrowed one not only has excess space alongside head, but boy has also lost top of skullpan.

course, to flatter each sitter. But the general effect should be the same—and on the light side. This is the only way to assure that every portrait on a page will be reproduced at top quality.

3. *Shoot in sharp focus, and retouch all portraits.* Soft or diffused focus is often the lazy or inept photographer's escape from painstaking self-discipline. He may like it; his sitters and your readers will not.

4. *Make all head sizes the same.* This is the only way to assure that all combinations of portraits will reproduce well and look attractive.

The image should be placed so that the nostrils are at, or a trifle above, the center of the picture. There should be a fairly generous margin at top and sides to avoid an uncomfortable jammed effect.

5. *Portraits should be checked against a Kodak Gray Scale.* The lightest area in a picture should be at the 10 percent mark of the scale. The deepest should be no darker than 90 percent. Lighter skin tones will look like the chalk makeup of a circus clown. Deep shadows under the eyes or nose and along the cheekbones will create a villainous appearance. There must be detail visible in even the deepest shadow areas.

Whites of eyes and teeth must be brilliant; white clothing must be lighter than skin tones.

Reproductions in your yearbook will not have quite as good quality as the original photograph, so originals must be of top quality. If any print fails to meet specifications, it should be returned to the photographer promptly for reprinting.

Most platemakers prefer *glossy prints* (*glossies*). A few feel that *dull-finish* prints give better results. You should find out your printer's preference and instruct the photographer—professional and student—to furnish that kind. Under no circumstances should the heavily textured *matte finish* be used. This is the kind the studio photographer usually furnishes his customers. The tiny hills and valleys of rough paper cast shadows that are reproduced on the printing plate.

Faculty Portraits

Because there are so many student portraits—even if only those of seniors are used—they must be standardized. But portraits of the faculty should be much more individualized. They should tell more than "This is how Miss Brown looks." They should "capture some of the spirit" and say "This is how Miss Brown is."

Dr. Daniel J. Moffie, School of Business

"Industrialists that I work with are always asking me whether our young people are prepared when they come out of college to go into industry.
I tell them yes, they have the potential, the ability, and are willing to work."

Dr. Ralph C. Patrick, Epidemiology and Anthropology, School of Public Health

"The General College should loosen up, now that there is greater variation in prior preparation. Placement should tailor requirements to fit needs."
"You have to require a certain amount of knowledge. But require knowledge, not courses."

CANDID PORTRAITS should always record characteristic pose of subject. But care must be taken that subject is never embarrassed by unplanned picture. Here teacher loses no dignity because of unorthodox perch and, twenty years later, reader will say, "Yes, that's the way I remember him!"

FACULTY PORTRAITS show teachers in action. Natural histrionics of interesting lecturer usually result in excellent candids as here. In addition to formal identification, each portrait is accompanied by quotation from teacher that further illumines his character or professional interests or attitudes.

AT-WORK CANDIDS are fine way of capturing subject to tell more of him than formal portrait might.

"POSED CANDIDS" combine best of both kinds of portraiture. By placing subject in appropriate setting and posing him in approximately position photographer wants, he can then wait till subject relaxes into some characteristic stance that has all informal pleasantness of true candid.

"MANIPULATED CANDIDS" require ingenuity by cameraman. Here student's position and pose could not be changed; she was tied to language-lab sound system, so photographer changed his position. He clicked shutter several times—without actually exposing film—until student ignored him. When he finally shot, result was this fine picture.

An excellent technique is that used on the covers of *Time* magazine. Here the background explains much about the person's activities, interests, and personality. Such backgrounds may be natural: A blackboard filled with equations for the geometry teacher; the fascinating equipment in the lab for the physics teacher; the casual array of books on shelves for an English instructor.

You may catch a teacher in a "posed candid" as he enjoys a hobby or does his daily chores. A teacher intent on grading papers will reveal more of her personality and dedication than when sitting for a formal portrait.

Group Portraits

Few yearbook jobs have a higher potential for staff headaches than the shooting of group pictures. Good planning—and good communications —can minimize the migraine.

Scheduling must be done well in advance, and groups should be notified at least four weeks before their sitting. Be specific on date, time, place, and costumes. There should be adequate time scheduled for making a good picture but none wasted between groups.

Necessary reshots require a week's advance appointment. If a group must postpone an appointment, it should give forty-eight hours' notice.

The photographer should be instructed to wait no more than ten minutes for tardy members. This will create a big uproar the first time; the Chemistry Club will insist that he wait for the missing vice-president. But when the picture is made—on schedule and without a full complement—the student body will get the message loud and clear. Other groups will be prompt and complete. But if you make an exception for one organization, all others will insist on the same privilege, and your schedule will soon disintegrate.

Group pictures will be best against plain, uniform backgrounds. Often the cameraman has suitable draperies; perhaps the drama department will lend you some. The staff can acquire its own. Inexpensive bedsheets in pastel colors—rather than white—can be sewn together (in the home ec class, perhaps) to provide the required area. Usually two or three different colors are required to make the most effective contrast between clothing—especially uniforms—and background.

If natural backgrounds are used, the photographer must beware of patterned wallpaper or draperies. The human eye usually ignores them. But in a picture, floral patterns grow out of heads like Medusa's snakes; light fixtures can transform a student into an elk as they appear to emerge from his head. Shiny painted or paneled walls will reflect lights and "burn out" an area of the picture. Pictures framed in glass are especially dangerous in this aspect—and so are oil paintings.

Posing a group takes skill—and time. Don't let

LOOSE POSING creates wasted space. In all group shots, space between heads, both vertically and horizontally, is wasted and must be minimized during posing. Diagram shows waste areas (lined) between heads and (by arrow) where cropping should be done.

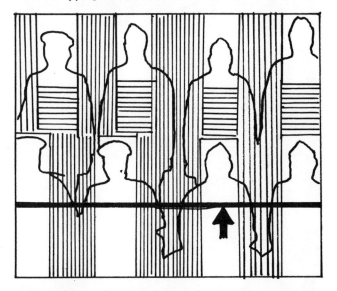

your subjects become bored during this necessary preparation.

Subjects must be arranged so that they stand much more closely together than they would naturally. Space between heads is always wasted in a picture; to minimize it, shoulders must overlap. Yet the posing should be "easy"; subjects should not stand stiffly or obviously crowded.

Remember that faces must be identified in the book; they should be arranged in what will be recognized as rows, although a little horizontal variation is pleasant. There should be minimum space between rows of faces. If tall boys stand behind short, seated girls, we will get too much shirt-and-jacket in the picture.

Athletic bleachers make good posing platforms.

GROUP PORTRAITS are made more appealing through unusual groupings, interesting background, or explanatory props.

For smaller groups, stairways and terraces are excellent. Even ladders can be used for the smallest groups.

Outdoor settings are pleasant, especially when even some of the group's activities are carried out there.

The smaller the group, the more informally it may be posed.

No matter what the size of the group, it should not be subdivided; it must "make just one picture." This is done by having everyone look at the same object. Often this is the camera. But with smaller groups, an appropriate prop can provide that unity of attention.

Let's suppose we are taking the sixteen-member Biology Club. We could have a grouping around a lab table, with everyone looking at a model of a plant. But if half the group looks at the model and the others look at a chart, the result will be "two pictures" that just happen to be on the same sheet of paper.

If the space between two people is much greater than that between other pairs, the composition will break apart at that point.

Interesting poses for smaller groups are those often called *surreal* or *abstract*. These are patently artificial poses, although there is an obvious, artistic reason for them. For example, we might put the backstage crew for the class play on the stage with the scenery turned backward. The subjects are posed at various levels, on obviously unnatural platforms. We might take two large ladders, posing one individual at the middle of one, another at the top of the second. Another student may sit on a plank supported by the ladders. Such posing is done to create a pleasant, abstract pattern, something like that of a Mondrian painting. Each student is dressed, or holds an object, to denote his job. The scene painter may have a big paintbrush; the electrician may hold a spotlight in his lap; the makeup girl a jar of cream and a powder puff.

Faculty members in such a grouping might use props to denote the subjects they teach. The geography teacher would hold a globe; the chemistry instructor a picturesque piece of glass equipment; the coach a football, and so on.

Such pictures can tell a story effectively, especially when many unrelated subjects must be depicted in one photograph. Besides, they are fun to pose and shoot.

The one pose to avoid is the horrible "picket fence," a row of people standing ramrod stiff against a wall . . . and wondering what to do with their hands.

Adequate and good lighting is essential to quality group shots. There must be at least two sources of front lighting, otherwise some people will look pale as death, and others will lurk in shadows. Front lighting must be uniform on every person.

The background must also be well lighted. The typical black background of front-flash pictures will make the pages of your book heavy and unattractive.

For outside group shots, avoid direct sunlight that casts deep shadows. *Open shade*—neither in dark shadows nor in full sun—gives the best results. Your subjects won't have to squint into glaring light. In fact, they won't even have to face directly into the sun if you use *fill-in flash*. This technique should be used on all posed *outdoor* shots to effect uniform lighting and capture good detail.

Atmosphere and Record

Atmosphere shots are unmatched for evoking memories. You will naturally want exterior shots of your school and its grounds. A shot down the main corridor as classes change tells a story that is familiar but cherished. So can the same corridor late in the afternoon, empty except for a lone custodian sweeping at the far end.

These are the arty shots that demand creativity and perception by the cameraman. Subjects, moods, and techniques are so varied that no book could even list them, much less make comment. All that can be said is that these pictures require much time and patience—as well as skill. They should be well planned, and adequate time for them must be allowed on the schedule.

Almost the same as atmosphere shots are *record* or *documentary photos*. These recall for the reader the details of familiar surroundings that all too soon grow hazy in memory. Even the most commonplace can be wrapped in a magic by the perceptive cameraman. No subject should be overlooked or rejected because it is familiar.

A typical classroom, a line of buses, the trophy case, the locker room, the art workshop . . . even the cafeteria line or the snack shop across the street. All these are part of our year at school and should be recorded.

Documentaries are not as moody as atmosphere shots. But they deserve the best from a photographer. Good record shots will be among the most cherished parts of any yearbook.

News Pictures

Every picture must tell a story. This may be a statement as simple as: "Spring brings flowers." But a news picture must be more specific. It must tell, as completely and interestingly as is possible, the details of a specific event.

Most news pictures for a yearbook report events that can be anticipated. The editor and cameraman must plan each picture in as great detail as they can. Not only the participants but the background must be shown to tell the story properly.

Suppose we are covering the Homecoming Game. Participants will be alumni, students, players, and the queen. If we can get all in one well-composed picture, we will tell the story properly. We can shoot from the press box or a high point. We can pose the queen with the president of the Alumni Association and the team captain with the stands in the background. We can shoot action on the field with the queen in the background. There are literally dozens of ways to tell the story.

The editor will tell the cameraman the basic shot to make. This is the photographer's first responsibility, to fulfill the editor's instructions. But often the unexpected makes the best picture; the cameraman must be alert for that, also.

Suppose that little dog—which seems to be standard equipment at every football game—starts chewing on the train of the queen's skirt. That shot couldn't possibly be anticipated; but it would certainly be an outstanding one. The photographer must be ready to make the unexpected picture.

On news assignments, the cameraman will always take *insurance shots.* Film is comparatively cheap; it is better to shoot two dozen pictures and eliminate twenty-three than to shoot only a couple and find they are unusable—with no chance to do them over.

The cameraman should study pictures of previous similar events. He should talk with participants beforehand. He should try to foresee the routine and be alert to potential variations.

If he is going to cover a play, he should attend rehearsals and note when the action of the drama creates an interesting grouping. If he is to cover a baseball game, he ought to know that a man on third is a potential scorer. The photographer will get to the left of home plate to record a possible squeeze play.

Above all, he must have his camera ready at all times, exposure set, shutter cocked and approximately in focus. When our defenseman intercepts a pass and scoots for the winning touchdown, there isn't time to do anything except lift the camera and shoot.

Picture Stories

Comparatively new in yearbook use is the technique of using a *picture story* or *essay* to add depth and interest to a yearbook. As its name indicates, a picture story is a narrative, a set of photos that progresses chronologically. The best subject is one that most of your readers have experienced. The "actors" should be played down so that the story becomes that of every student, not just one or two.

Suppose we are doing a story on College Board exams. It might start with a student studying, the night before. The next morning he's too nervous to eat breakfast. He looks over his notes for the last time as he walks into school. We see him pondering and working on his paper. The clock shows that it's quitting time—but his face tells us that he still has many unanswered questions. We might conclude with him drowning his sorrows—or celebrating—with a milkshake and comparing notes with classmates. We might even have a P.S. on the day he receives his scores.

One of the most charming picture stories your author has seen shows only shoes. Sneaker-clad male and female feet walk up toward the school and along the corridor. They meet at the water fountain and under a cafeteria table. But now comes calamity! The male feet turn toward a very feminine pair of high heels; the female sneakers twist in anguish as they are left alone. Then, at home, those feet slip into a pair of silvery slippers wreathed in a frothy formal skirt. They join a pair of patent leather slippers on the dance floor, and the final shot shows those feet, on tiptoes, facing and close to the boy's. Happy ending.

Because faces are never shown, each reader can almost literally put himself—or herself—into the pictured shoes.

Picture stories can be used anywhere in the book. They are ideal for adding contrast and interest to the seniors' portrait section, for instance.

The story can be spread across several pages or be complete on a single page or spread.

Picture Essays

The picture essay, like the familiar essay, doesn't say "This is what happened." Instead, it says, "This is what I feel about something." A good essay makes a photographic statement and explores it in one or more shots. Then it makes the

OUT-OF SEASON PICTURES can be interesting. Here staff was faced with problem of illustrating lacrosse article although season didn't start till long after book deadline. Because sport was new to school, there weren't even last-year pictures in files. So this fanciful "portrait" was created. Technique can be used for any activity—baseball, track, field days and commencement—that are planned for after yearbook deadlines.

same statement, or varies it a little, and explores that facet. This continues until the final shot reprises the whole essay.

Suppose our subject is "Track practice is self-discipline." The first shot shows a runner, all by himself, straining without the exhilaration of competition or applause. A couple more shots show the loneliness of a boy competing only against his own previous performance. The second key shot shows him in calisthenics with a corroborating shot of practicing starts. The next key is the complete weariness with which he walks to the locker room. The final shot shows him recording his best time on his performance chart.

Subject matter for photographic essays is as wide as for literary essays. By recording emotions as well as events, picture essays increase the reader's pleasure each time he studies them.

Candids

Candid photos are unposed, as are most news pictures, but their subject matter is less momentous. The good candid is a slice of actual life; its appeal is in its unstudied authenticity. The best candid is the one that captures a person completely unaware of the camera. Because all of us are hams to some degree, we tend to pose, to "act," when we see a camera pointed at us. We never look completely natural.

The candid cameraman must therefore shoot unobtrusively. He must recognize a good picture in the split second that it unfolds, yet he still must plan ahead.

The photographer will study the people whom he hopes to capture in candids. He will look for characteristic positions and actions. He will seek a vantage point that will make for good composition without sacrificing spontaneity and naturalness. This planning will result in far better candids than the technique of just shooting so many pictures that the law of averages will produce a usable one.

Semicandids combine posing for good pictorial composition with unselfconscious action by the subject. The cameraman might set up an easel in the art room so that the background is appropriate or the subject is pleasingly framed. Then he will wait till the artist becomes so engrossed in his work that he completely ignores the camera. Then he makes the posed candid.

A variation is the *posed-action* shot, used most frequently on the athletic field. The cameraman may have a football player run along a determined path to catch a pass thrown to a specific point. The action can be anticipated, but the player will be concentrating so much on catching the ball that his actions will—at least after two or three dry runs—be unstudied and spontaneous.

For most candids, the cameraman need not take many insurance shots. He can always go back tomorrow and reshoot. Only if the action is one that cannot conveniently be taken again, will he shoot insurance.

Lines of Force

No matter what kind of pictures he is shooting, the photographer will seek certain qualities that are always necessary.

A basic principle of layout is that "Pictures must

CHARACTER SKETCH blends quotations from subject with candid shots made during interview. Only person with interesting facial expressions and gestures should be chosen for this treatment. Otherwise editor must "use same picture twice" . . . or three or four times.

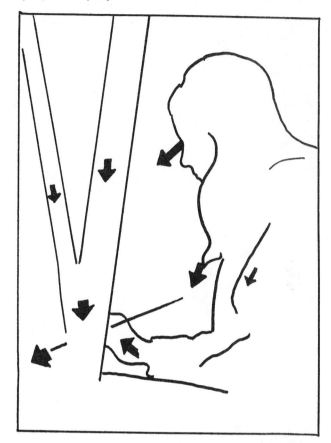

face into the page," so the cameraman must make sure to shoot pictures facing both left and right. It is impossible to do a good layout when all available pictures "point" in only one direction.

If possible, two photographers should be assigned to all athletic and news events that cannot be reshot. They should be on opposite sides of the field or action. Then one will take a touchdown run toward the left while his partner will record the same play moving to the right.

Strong action in a picture creates a *line of force*, a certain momentum that carries the reader's eye along in the direction of the movement. Perhaps that movement need not be as powerful as a fullback diving into the line. It may be as subtle as the gaze of a person; the reader wants to know what the subject is looking at and looks in the same direction.

Most pictures have built-in "arrows" that create lines of force. If the subject is pointing, the reader will look that way as readily as he follows the index finger of an actual person.

Arrows may be far less obtrusive. The human body forms many of them in any picture. Fingers, arms, elbows, and legs are arrows. So are the folds of clothing. Any strong line in a picture carries the eye with it. If such a line doesn't have an "arrowhead" to indicate direction of movement, the eye will follow it downward and to the right as it naturally moves in reading. Two or more lines

that tend to converge, even if they don't meet within the picture, suggest an arrowhead, and create a line of force.

The cameraman must arrange these lines of force to move in the direction required by a layout. Or he must make his shots so the layout man will have at least one picture with the arrow pointing in the proper direction.

Harmony

Harmony is a pleasant repetition of shapes and patterns, in the same picture or in a set of them.

The classical *pattern shot* is a good demonstration of harmony. This may be the neat rows of chairs just before study hall opens, a series of test tubes in the chem lab, the lines of bleachers, or the repetition of architectural elements in your school building.

Harmony may come from commonality of subject matter. It might show various methods of transportation used by students to get to school. It might be a series on students eating . . . pizza at a corner stand, soup in the cafeteria, candy bars in the corridor, or a sandwich as a student reads a

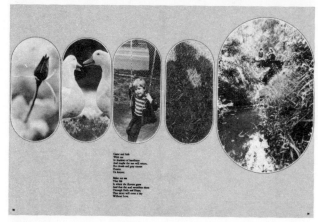

HARMONY OF SHAPES is created by repetition of oval motif. Then drastic change of size as here (or it could have been in shape) adds accent that heightens reader's pleasure.

textbook on the front steps.

Harmony may be a repetition of similar—but not exactly alike—forms: a boy standing beside a statue in the lobby; a girl cheerleader leaping just as a basketball player does; a hundred mouths open in ecstasy as the winning score is made.

In the yearbook, every picture must have a harmonious relation to all other pictures, especially those on the same page or spread, but also throughout the book.

HARMONY IN SUBJECT MATTER pleases reader. Whether photographer arranged this picture or was lucky enough to capture candid, studying figure reminds us of Great Emancipator reading by light of fireplace.

HARMONY OF SHAPES combines same basic forms—bodies of football players—with enough variations among individual shapes to create interest. (Charles Thiele is photographer.)

Same repetition of unchanging forms—tables and lights—with variation in shapes of studying students makes harmonious and appealing library scene.

HARMONY OF LAYOUT comes from repetition of forms and subject. Four full pages of this book depict passing of seasons on campus. These two are for fall and winter. Lonely figure against vast open background in each picture repeats familiar motif. Variations on theme come from different weather depicted and by placement of figure in different corners.

Contrast

When the brass horns have dominated "The Stars and Stripes Forever," we are delighted to have the piccolos swirl their sparkling, pointed notes. After a heavy dinner we enjoy a light dessert. Just so the reader likes contrast in pictures.

Useful *contrast* comes from variation in shapes. Most pictures are close to a 3 × 5 ratio; long, thin pictures, whether horizontal or vertical, give pleasant variety.

If most of the pictures on a spread are light in tone, a dark one will be the change of pace that adds interest. And vice versa, of course.

Contrast comes from changing camera angle. The photographer should climb to a high vantage point or get down on the floor so the bird's-eye—or worm's-eye—view will contrast with the conventional shoulder-level picture.

Contrast comes from camera range. A long, overall shot or an extreme closeup gives good variety to the middle-range shots that represent such a large part of the pictures in most yearbooks.

Subject matter offers contrast, too. Pair a shot of your school after a heavy snowfall with a picture, taken from the same spot, in midsummer. Shoot from the auditorium to the stage; then shoot from the stage down into the seats. Show a smiling cheerleader after a winning game and the same girl after you've lost a heartbreaker.

Contrast is most dramatic, and pleasant, when the reader has been led to expect one thing and is surprised with another. A classic shot is that of a large group of graduates listening to an outdoor commencement address. Their mortarboards create a rhythmic pattern shot. Row after row, the

CONTRAST COMES from playing horizontal shape of picture at left against vertical mass of one at right and by intersecting angles of instruments themselves.

In any page layout, useful contrast can be obtained by using pictures that depart greatly from customary 3x5 ratio. Tall, skinny pictures or wide, shallow ones, as well as providing contrast, add "dynamic thrust" to page.

squares create a formal checkerboard. But what's this! Here one of the cap-and-gowned figures is sound asleep. The contrast of his position and the droop of his cap catches us up sharply . . . and then we smile in appreciation of the unexpected. Can you visualize it? And you're smiling, aren't you?

Kinds of Photographs

The most common picture in a yearbook is a *square halftone*. This is any rectangular picture; it need not be square but the corners must all be 90 degrees.

A variation is to cut a picture into a *rhomboid*.

DISORIENTATION IN READING results when facing pages switch from conventional horizontal format to sideways, landscaped one. Compare this unpleasant contrast with that shown above, which at first glance may seem closely similar but retains horizontal orientation of vertical photo.

The top and bottom may be horizontal with the sides parallel to each other but not at right angles to top and bottom. Or the sides may be vertical with top and bottom parallel but not horizontal.

Pictures may be circular, oval, diamond-shaped, or in free form. These shapes are difficult to work into a pleasant layout, and their use is quite rare today. Because these forms were so popular a couple of decades ago, they have a distinctly old-fashioned flavor that few staffs want in their yearbook.

If the entire background is eliminated from a picture, the result is a *silhouette*. If the tone of a picture fades almost imperceptibly into the white of the paper, it is a *vignette*. If it has one or more straight sides, the picture is a *modified silhouette* or modified vignette.

A section cut out of a photograph is a *mortice*. *External mortices* are cut into the edge of a photo. The most common is the *notch*, a rectangle cut out of a corner of the photo. An *internal mortice* is an opening entirely within the photo.

Most mortices are created by straight cuts, although the opening may be made by curves. The openings of mortices may hold type or another photo.

Mortices should be used only to remove useless areas from a picture. If any necessary detail is removed by a mortice, the technique has not been used wisely. Never use a mortice just to link two photos together.

Sometimes a striking effect can be obtained by unusual cropping. Such dramatic cropping is useful when the staff is forced to use a picture that has often appeared in print and, especially, when it is impossible to shoot the picture from a different angle.

Great care must be exercised that such unconventional cropping does not destroy the communicative value of the photo. If the reader is confused by such cropping, he will not be pleased or informed.

Special Effects

Photographs are reproduced in printing by breaking them down into a pattern of very fine dots of various sizes; this is the *halftone* principle.

But halftones can be created by other patterns, too. A familiar one is *parallel lines* that thin or swell to give the effect of various tones of gray. *Concentric circles* produce the same halftone effect.

Other special screens have patterns of irregular dots, shapes, and sizes that create a *mezzotint* effect.

All these effects are produced by *special screens*. Few platemakers can furnish all of the great many of these unconventional screens, so the editor must check to determine what is available for his use.

"MOSAIC CROPPING" is useful when previously published picture must be used again. Here editor made "new" picture from commencement shot of year before by cropping to accentuate diagonal files of graduates.

of time. Syracuse looked as if it was all they could do to keep them from scoring with it. The quarterback passed for one touchdown to make it 15-12 and almost got another, except that Hal Rooney intercepted. Before more embarrassment could take place, the game ended.

The powerful Richmond squad dropped by for an official scrimmage and became the Orange's third shutout victim, which surprised nobody. In an unparalleled mood of sadism, Ben Schwartzwalder played his sophomores, but the spirited Spider defense held them to under 51 points.

Rich King, showing remarkable calm in the situation, completed seven of 12 passes for 212 yards, and in four carries Bo Nance did the work of three clipping penalties. Touchdowns were scored by Nance, Mike Koski, Dick Bowman, Bill Schoonover, Ray Free, George Kontrabecki and John Snider. John Paglio kicked six extra points, and

"MOSAIC CROPPING" is useful tool for editor when used properly. Here vertical action of basketball is emphasized by cutting photo into vertical panels, then raising jumping figure.

This book is in "landscaped format," pages run sideways with gutter at top or bottom, rather than at side, of pages. Landscaping adds to cost of binding and (as author can testify after going through pages of this book) is awkward and tiring for reader to handle.

"MOSAIC CROPPING" eliminates most of confusing background of grandstands by breaking original picture into three separate elements. Football had been almost invisible against background of original. Relative position of passer, ball, and receiver remains constant.

In this sports section, running copy has been used to narrate entire football season.

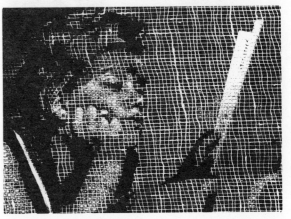

"SPECIAL SCREENS" add variety, especially to divider pages where mood is more important than photographic detail. Basketball player is in "posterized" technique, football player in "steel engraving" screen.

"Concentric circle" pattern is used for portrait of girl. (If center of circles were at one eye, effect would be even more striking.) Studying girl is printed with "filagrave" screen and one of archway is in "slantweave."

On conventional halftones, dots are so fine that they are practically invisible. But there are times when dramatic effects can be achieved by exaggerating the dot pattern. A photo is made into a halftone, let's say, of 2 × 3 inches with 55 lines of dots per linear inch. The proof of this halftone is then enlarged to the desired size. The increase also enlarges the individual dots so that they become readily apparent to the naked eye.

Such *blowup halftones* should be used only for pictures that have no fine detail, as the coarser the dot pattern, the less detail is reproduced.

An interesting technique is to reproduce a photo as a *line cut*. This process is called *line conversion* or *linear definition*. This requires a high-contrast print, with deep blacks and sheer whites. Intermediate tones of gray will be eliminated in the platemaking. The result looks like a pen-and-ink drawing or a linoleum block. Much detail is lost in this process, and the photo to be treated this way must be chosen so the black areas define all the shapes. Such art should be marked: *Make Line Cut of This*.

An extension of line conversion is *posterization*. Here the myriad gray tones in a photograph are simplified to black, white, and a 50 percent gray. This process is more expensive than line conversion but is a very effective one.

Another interesting technique that comes under the broad umbrella of *photomechanics* is a distorting of colors. This may be done by the photog-

Identical photos of building use "vertagrave" for upper one and "crossline" for lower.

Many platemakers give their own names to such special screens, and editor should be careful to designate his choice by terms used by his own printer rather than by those given here.

"LINEAR CONVERSION," also called "line definition," makes this interesting divider-page grouping. Care must be taken that no significant photographic detail is lost when middle grays are converted into solid blacks or white. In lower photo, for instance, horn player's profile has been lost in conversion. Reenforcing crucial lines in photo with India ink or black crayon ensures against such loss.

"ZOOM-IN EFFECT" is produced by enlarging and repeating portion of photo. Here two tiny figures are first shown on vastness of stage where they are speaking. Then details are shown in closer view inset into lower-right corner. Effect would be even stronger if original shot had been used for inset.

rapher in the darkroom; *solarization* is one of the variations. Another is to use the conventional color plates (which are described in detail in Chapter 6) but print a different hue with them. The blue plate, for instance, might be printed with yellow ink. Thus every element in the original picture that appears as blue would be yellow in the reproduction. The sky would obviously be distorted; so would foliage and human skin tones. Any hue that contains blue would change appearance; violet (made of blue and red) would become orange (yellow and red), for instance.

Whatever manipulation is done with photographs and/or color should always be done with great care and in a way that the resulting loss of detail or of distortion will not rob the picture of "the essence of truth."

A *reverse* of a photo looks like a negative film viewed against strong light. This technique reverses values; whites become black and vice versa.

The term "reverse" is often misused to designate a picture that is printed so that it faces right instead of left. Reversing of direction is technically *flopping*. To make sure, all pictures to be reversed should be marked: REVERSE, *change blacks to white*. Pictures that are to be flopped should be marked: FLOP, *reverse direction*.

Flopping is dangerous. If there is a definite "right-handedness" to a picture—a person writing, signs, pocket handkerchiefs, etc.—there obviously can be no flopping. But even pictures that are not as clearly oriented have a built-in right and left. Often the flopping of such a photo creates a feeling of vague annoyance in the reader. Only under the most dire need should the editor even consider flopping.

Hand Art

Hand art is any that is not produced by a camera. It affords pleasant contrast to photography and, though its use is most frequent on title and divider pages, small *spots* can be used to enliven any page.

Pen-and-ink is a favorite. It is done by pen or brush with black India ink on white or bluish-white drawing paper or board. The drawing is usually 50 percent wider than the image will appear in print. Such drawings are best when most simple. Very fine lines are apt to clog up when the platemaker reduces the drawing.

Pen-and-ink can be combined with photography for interesting results.

Texture may be added to pen-and-ink—*line work*—by *spatter* or dabbing with a sponge. Another technique is to use *shading sheets*. These are self-adhesive plastic on which is printed patterns of dots or lines. The desired shape is cut out of the sheet with a needlelike stylus and laid on the drawing. A clear, waxy backing on the sheet adheres it to the drawing when it is *burnished*, polished down with a smooth tool. A gray effect is thus produced to add interest to the basic black and white.

Collages are art created by pasting together various materials of interesting texture or tonal value. Collages can also be made by pasting together photographs. These are frequently misnamed as *montages*. A real montage is a print made by exposing several negatives to a single sheet of photo paper.

Photographic collages and montages rarely produce pleasant results; usually they are busy and confusing, and their use had best be avoided.

Paintings, in *oil, watercolor, casein,* or *gouache,* can make interesting illustrations. Although the original art can be sent to the printer, there is danger that it may be damaged; it is best to make a good photograph of the original. This not only protects the art, it also enables the editor to see how well a full-color original will reproduce in black and white.

Crayon drawings reproduce well, especially if they are done on a *toothy,* heavily textured, paper. Blending or smearing the crayon creates an unpleasant effect in most instances.

Pencil drawings are difficult to reproduce, and it is wise to disregard this technique for yearbook use.

Block prints are striking. They are cut from wood, linoleum, sponges, erasers, or even potatoes. The little "accidentals," small overlooked areas that print inadvertently add pleasant informality that cannot be duplicated in any other medium, although sometimes an artist will try to give the effect of a block print in an ink drawing.

Three-dimensional art is pleasant and can add unusual interest to a yearbook. *Sculpture* in *clay, papier-mâché,* or *paper* offers a wide range of techniques, each with an appeal of its own. Such art must be photographed to produce platemaking copy. Proper lighting requires great skill on the part of the cameraman.

There is no need to discuss the techniques of

CARTOONS MAKE pleasant accent against photographs, which predominate in all yearbooks. They are also pleasant way to add humor, which is often lacking. Caricaturist who can retain likeness of his subjects (as at right) is staffer to be cherished.

THE RED AND BLACK

Semi-Weekly Campus Newspaper

"CROPPER'S L'S" are useful device for helping editor visualize different "pictures" within single "photograph." By forming rectangles of various proportions and sizes over photograph, editor could in this case find at least three pleasant, usable compositions: vertical one with model, man, and start of sculpture; one shown here; horizontal one with all four people.

hand art in this book. There are many excellent books on the subject that you can borrow from your art teacher. Besides, the topic is so vast it would take the contents of a five-foot shelf—not a book of this size—to explore it adequately.

The staff should demand the same superior quality from hand art as it does of photography. High school artists are usually in early development of their talents and it isn't every year that one with enough skill is available. Unless there is an outstanding artist on the staff, it is wise to stick to photography.

Cropping

Just as an editor improves written copy by careful editing, so he improves a photograph by *cropping*. Both processes increase the effectiveness of communication by eliminating distracting or unnecessary details.

Cropping a photograph increases its impact by

focusing all the reader's attention to those elements—and only those elements—that tell the story. The professional photo editor calls this "finding the picture in the photo."

Cropper's L's are a useful tool in finding the picture. These are L-shaped pieces of cardboard about an inch wide, which, when used in pairs, form rectangles of varying size and proportion. The editor tries out many possibilities until he finds the shape and area that include only the essentials of the picture.

The subject matter determines effective cropping. If the shot is of a vaulter going over the bar, you will leave enough sky to enhance the effect of height. If the picture is of a delicate physics experiment, you will crop out most of the student's body, concentrating on his hands and the apparatus.

If the subject is moving swiftly, leave room in the picture in front of him so that he doesn't bump

into the edge. Cropping close to the front of a subject gives an oppressive feeling of constriction.

"Crop ruthlessly!" is good advice. "Never shave; slash!" is the way one professional puts it. Your reader should always know that you have cropped deliberately; if he gets the feeling that you "just slipped," cropping is irritating.

If you don't want to show the whole head of a person, don't just slice a thin layer off his skull, come to the middle of his forehead.

Don't crop at a body joint—ankle, knee, wrist, elbow, or shoulder. It looks like an amputation. Never guillotine a subject by cropping at his neck—always include a little of his shoulders. You may, if the subject requires, crop into the chin, just below the lips.

Crop standing subjects at about the bottom of their rib cage. Full-length figures are rarely attractive or informative unless their costumes are un-

PROPER CROPPING eliminates dead areas in photo. Here cropping should be at point of arrow. Exactly half of this picture is utterly wasted—empty bleachers add neither charm nor information. Had the team been arranged in eight rows instead of four, picture could have remained full-page wide (as now), but each face would be twice as wide as it is now.

usual. Seated subjects, especially female, should be taken, or cropped, so their legs don't show. Nothing is more sloppy than a set of ankles crossed at varying angles, especially if they display a band of skin between socktops and trousers. When their owner sits, women's calves are often flattened to proportions a fullback might envy.

CREATIVE CROPPING helps even good photo. Both original pictures here (above) were attractive in square shape, although squares are static and usually less interesting. Cropping to vertical form gives editors choice of two shapes in creating interesting layout.

EXAMPLE I.

37 picas WIDE
PAGE 107 #2
LOGBOOK

CROPPING PICTURE removes unessential as, here, upper quarter, foreground, and useless strips at sides. "Crop marks" are drawn with grease pencil in margins and can readily be erased and redrawn.

Projecting tab—often furnished by printer—tells how wide cropped picture is to be in printed form. Page and position (#2) are noted and—very important—yearbook is identified. Thousands of photos come to printer every day; those not identified with specific book are easily misplaced.

Dimension of printing plate may also be given by writing it in bottom margin, between crop marks, and extending arrows from these instructions outward to those marks.

Editor should not specify both new width and height. When this photo is reduced to 37 picas wide, it will reduce at same ratio up-and-down. Should editor specify new height that is different from what platemaking process creates, confusion sets in. Platemaker then doesn't know whether to follow new-width or new-height instructions and may cut off plate arbitrarily . . . and in manner not satisfactory to editor.

Never allow any lingerie to show in a picture. An exposed shoulder strap mars the appearance of a well-groomed girl. The cameraman should check the subject to avoid such problems; if any do occur, they must be removed from the picture by blacking out with India ink or poster paint.

Cropping can be done by actually cutting the photo to the desired area. But this is dangerous; if you change your mind or the cutter slips, the photo is ruined and you will require a new one. This is costly in time and money.

Cropping is best done by *crop marks* in the margin of the print; they show the area the platemaker should use. If crop marks are made with grease pencil, they can easily be removed with a tissue if there is a change of plans. The complete photo can be filed for future use after marks are removed.

A typical cropped photo is shown in Example I. Marks at the bottom indicate the vertical portion of the photo that is to be used; the single mark at

the right indicates a horizontal "cut." When there are no crop marks, the printer will go clear to the margin.

The size of the engraving, as it will appear in print, is written between the appropriate crop marks. Be sure that this is the dimension of the reproduction. Often an editor will make crop marks, measure the distance between them, and write that figure—rather than the new dimension. In that case, the reproduction will be the same size as the original. If it is supposed to be the same size, the instructions are written as S/S or SAME SIZE.

Another way of indicating cropping is by an overlay of transparent tracing paper. The desired area is drawn in grease pencil, with a light touch to avoid damage to the emulsion. The overlay is especially useful to indicate where silhouetting or morticing is to be done.

The least desirable—though very common—way of showing crops is to hold the photo against a window (this becomes the equivalent of the useful but not vital *light table*) and drawing the desired rectangle on the back of the photo. Great care must be taken that the writing does not indent the emulsion of the picture.

PROPER CROPPING does not always mean elimination of foreground and/or background. Here rolling woods behind group and sand traps in front add significant detail and beauty to picture of golf team. Inexperienced or over-enthusiastic editor might be tempted to crop at notches.

In all instances a flap may be attached to carry instructions.

Scaling

Rarely is the original photograph the exact size as it will appear in the yearbook. The editor usually works with 8 × 10 glossies, so he must *scale* each picture to determine the area it will occupy in print. Most pictures are reduced; the plate-maker prefers it this way because when he *shoots down*, imperfections in the glossy are reduced.

The editor may use plain arithmetic to determine the size of the reproduction. The proportion of reduction of vertical dimensions will be identical to that of the width; so the formula is:

$$W : H = w : h$$

The capitals are the width (always given first) and height of the glossy; the small letters are dimensions of the reproduction.

The editor must know one of the new dimensions; this will usually be the width (although it can be the height). Suppose we have a glossy that, after cropping, measures 4½ inches wide by 7½ high. We want to determine how tall it will be when reduced to 3 inches in width. Our formula works like this:

$$W : H = w : h$$
$$4.5 : 7.5 = 3 : x$$
$$4.5x = 22.5$$
$$x = 5$$

(As you know from ninth-grade algebra, the "product of the means equals the product of the extremes"; you multiply the outside numbers and then the ones closest to the equal sign.)

This problem came out in neat numbers. But too often the result is an unwieldy fraction that we can't even find on our ruler. Therefore the professional picture editor utilizes the *common-diagonal method* for scaling. It is by far the best because it shows the actual shape and size of the reduction.

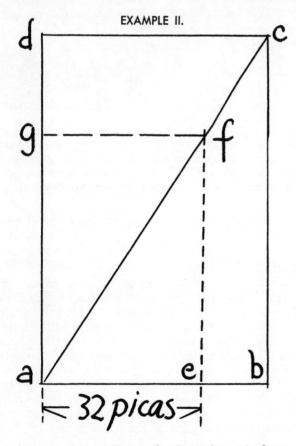

EXAMPLE II.

Assume that in Example II, an 8 × 10 glossy is to be reduced to 32 picas wide. Draw the diagonal *ac*. Along the bottom, measure off the desired width, 32 picas. At *e* erect a perpendicular till it hits the diagonal at *f*. Draw the horizontal from *f*

to *g*. The reduced picture will have the area *aefg*. We have only to measure *ag* to know the new height. But even before that, we saw the actual new size. If it looks too small—or too large—we have merely to select a different new width.

The same method works on those less frequent occasions when we know the desired height and must find the new width. In Example III, we have the same 8 × 10 glossy to be reduced to 42 picas tall. Draw the diagonal *hj*. Measure the desired height, *hl*. Draw the perpendicular, *lm*, and drop the parallel, *mn*. The new area is *hnml* and the new width is *hn*.

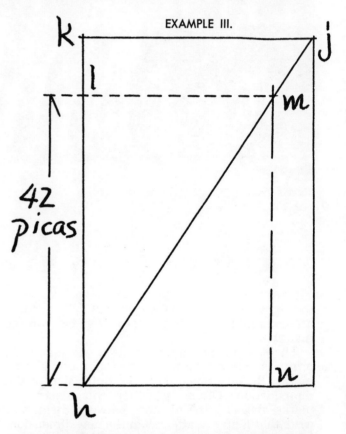

EXAMPLE III.

We must remember to use only the area left by cropping, not the whole glossy. In Example IV, crop marks in the margin mean that the platemaker will use only the area *opqr*. If we want this area to be 22 picas wide, draw the diagonal *oq*. Measure 22 picas, *os*. Draw the perpendicular, *st*, and the parallel, *tu*. The reduced picture will be *ostu*.

Once in a great while, the editor will need a reduction that must have two new dimensions in order to fit into a layout. The common-diagonal method works here, too. Look at Example V.

Here the editor has an 8 × 10 glossy that must be reduced to 18 × 30 picas to fit into a page. We draw the dimensions of the reduction, *vwxy*, and the diagonal *vx*, extending it to the margin of the photo at *z*.

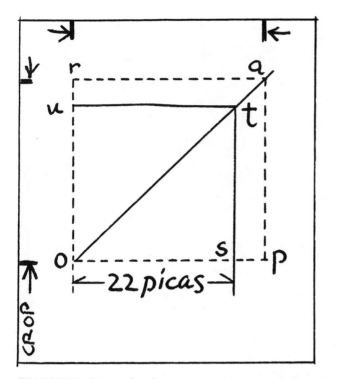

EXAMPLE IV. Picture has been cropped to area indicated. Scaling after cropping is demonstrated here.

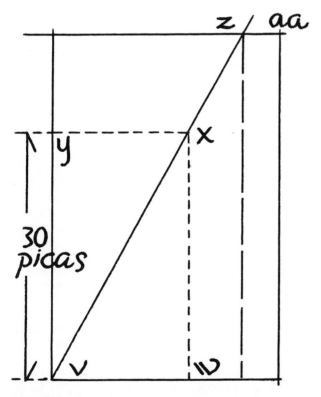

EXAMPLE V. Scaling and cropping to produce rectangle of specific height and width is demonstrated here.

Immediately we see that the dimensions of the original are out of proportion to those of the desired area. The glossy is too wide, by the distance of *z* to *aa*. To get the desired proportions in the reduction, the glossy must be narrowed. We can crop at *z* if the photo looks well that way. Or we may take the same amount—*z-aa*—off the left margin. Or we can take part off the left and the rest off the right. The method has shown us how much we must crop; we must use our judgment on where to crop.

Scaling may be done on an overlay or by drawing the exact dimensions of the cropped picture on another piece of paper.

Mechanical devices that resemble a simple slide rule (often they are in disc form) can also be used; but the common-diagonal is the simplest and easiest besides giving an instant visual answer.

Care of Art

All art is fragile and must be handled with care.

Hand art, especially, should be protected with an *overflap*, a sheet of bond or tracing paper and a sheet of heavier kraft paper. These are fastened to the back of the work and then folded over the front.

All art should be shipped flat. Rolling will produce breaks—especially on photos—that will be exaggerated in reproduction.

Obviously no art can ever be folded.

Photographs are easily bruised. If you write on the back of a picture, do it very lightly and only with a grease pencil or a felt-tip pen. (Be sure, however, that this is not a marker that may seep through the paper.) A regular pencil or ballpoint pen will raise the *emulsion* on the front of the photo. Even though it may be almost invisible to the eye, the intense lights of the platemaker will make the flaw a glaring one in reproduction.

Be careful that you do not write on a piece of paper that is lying on a photo. Even through one or more thicknesses of copy paper, such pressure can mar the emulsion.

The best method of conveying written instructions is to paste a *flap* or *tab* to the picture. This may be one so small that it carries only necessary instructions or it may be large enough that when it is folded back upon the glossy it will protect the delicate surface.

If a photo is warped, rewash and dry it. Trying to smooth out a tightly rolled photo will crack the emulsion.

Avoid fingerprints on photos. Even though you can't see them, the platemaker's camera can, and they will show when printed.

Never put a paper clip on a piece of art. Instead, paste the paper to the back of the work so that the written matter projects below; it can be folded over for shipment.

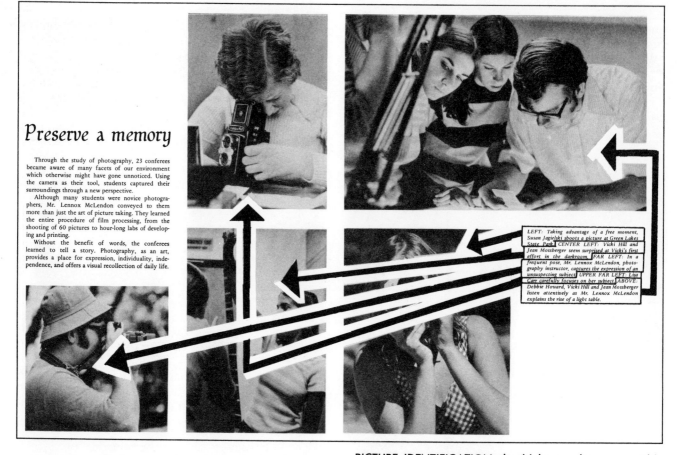

Preserve a memory

Through the study of photography, 23 conferees became aware of many facets of our environment which otherwise might have gone unnoticed. Using the camera as their tool, students captured their surroundings through a new perspective.

Although many students were novice photographers, Mr. Lennox McLendon conveyed to them more than just the art of picture taking. They learned the entire procedure of film processing, from the shooting of 60 pictures to hour-long labs of developing and printing.

Without the benefit of words, the conferees learned to tell a story. Photography, as an art, provides a place for expression, individuality, independence, and offers a visual recollection of daily life.

LEFT: Taking advantage of a free moment, Susan Jagielski shoots a picture at Green Lakes State Park. CENTER LEFT: Vicki Hill and Jean Mossberger seem surprised at Vicki's first effort in the darkroom. FAR LEFT: In a frequent pose, Mr. Lennox McLendon, photography instructor, captures the expression of an unsuspecting subject. UPPER FAR LEFT: Lisa Carr carefully focuses on her subject. ABOVE: Debbie Howard, Vicki Hill and Jean Mossberger listen attentively as Mr. Lennox McLendon explains the rise of a light table.

Package all art work between corrugated heavy board. Have the ribs on one running vertically and on the other crossways, for maximum protection. All such packages should be marked PHOTOGRAPHS—DO NOT BEND! Bright red labels with such copy can be bought at any stationery store and are well worth the few cents they cost.

Identification of Pictures

But even when the finest art has been handled in the most skillful and conscientious manner, the job is only half done. Because:

Every picture must be identified in type!

If an editor will heed only one hint in this book, this is the one that can make the most significant improvement in his work. It is the failure to identify pictures that lowers the value of countless yearbooks and eliminates the value entirely in some.

(A short time ago one of the most prestigious women's colleges produced a book exclusively of pictures. There was no type at all. It was as frustrating to friends and families as it was to the graduates: This was any college or no college; certainly it wasn't *their* college. The pictures could have been hanging in a gallery in Minnesota or published in a magazine in Milan. Certainly it captured no memories for future years. After the first

PICTURE IDENTIFICATION should be as close as possible to picture. Here, because all captions are ganged into single block, reader must first divide written copy into individual parts, then link words and pictures. As diagram shows, this becomes complicated. Then reader becomes weary and loses much of pleasure that pictures ought to provide.

perusal, when the scenes were still fresh and no *aide-mémoire* was required, the book was as impersonal as a stranger's photo file. The editor had failed. Unfortunately she had wasted not only her own time and effort, but also that of the staff as well as the money of the purchasers and from the class treasury that had subsidized the book.)

The author conducts workshops and seminars for student staffs throughout the whole upper portion of North America. And whenever he makes this statement, "Every picture must be identified!," he looks around for a deep hole in which he might hide, as he knows that he will immediately be the target of a veritable barrage of dissent.

After many years he is still puzzled by the vehemence of student editors on this topic. In all creative efforts there must be differences of opinion. Do we use Bodoni or Bulmer type? Do we use running heads? Should we have a white cover or a black one? Should we publish in spring or summer or even fall? But rarely are tempers as instantaneous or calorific as when the subject of picture identification comes to the agenda.

Let's examine the situation and test the validity of the admonition that: *Every picture must be identified!*

In a recent survey, a group of alumni of a fairly small high school were tested five years after graduation. Their class was of a size that each student knew some 90 percent of his classmates personally and could greet practically every one of others by name during their school years.

Yet in only those few years, memories had grown so rusty that they could identify only about 40 percent of their classmates' pictures, and of that group, approximately half could not be identified by their academic or extracurricular activities.

If this much erosion of memory takes place in the first five years, think of how bad it will be at the end of a decade. Or in the case of a larger graduating class when no one in the group knew everyone else even during their mutual schooldays!

Surely nothing is as frustrating and boring as looking at a group of pictures of people you don't know! In this case, then, the book has lost much —maybe all—of its value as a record.

The same thing also applies to supposedly re-

"SKETCH IDENTIFICATION" is useful when subjects do not form neat rows. In the outline drawing numbers are placed that match up with those in caption.

Religion

1—Most honor students rush home
2—Kathy Cole and Sidney Kaine
3—Ellen Campbell, Jane Shultz, Steve Horning, Sherri August
4—Linda Ecker and Brad Bryant
5—Bob Moore, Ralph Wilkinson, Charles Williams, Brad Bryant, Ed Dobiac
6—Michael Davidson and Albert Nurse
7—Michael Davidson
8—Ellen Campbell
9—Linda Ecker
10—Jeanne McConnell
11—Brad Bryant, all upstate football player caught in an outstanding play.

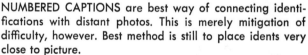

NUMBERED CAPTIONS are best way of connecting identifications with distant photos. This is merely mitigation of difficulty, however. Best method is still to place idents very close to picture.

cord shots. Without a caption, a photo might be an exuberant group of students celebrating a state athletic championship, it might be a belligerent invasion of your campus by some crosstown rival school, it might be a protest against cafeteria menus.

Thus every picture must be identified. (The repetition of this phrase is not from careless syntax; it seeks to emphasize the great importance of captions.) The caption should tell: This is the occasion this picture records; these are the people in the picture; this is something significant or interesting in the picture that the reader would overlook or not recognize if he were not told about it.

Whether to use a caption or just an ident is determined by the context. If you are devoting a whole spread to the Homecoming football game, the page copy block will carry all the 5 W's of the game, and, in most instances, captions can carry the pictures. But if you have a single *wild picture,* one that runs with no supporting story, then you will need *cutlines,* a lengthy kind of caption.

"But what about mood shots?" the student editor will demand. "Here I want to convey atmosphere, not specific information."

Let's analyze that situation. Obviously there are pictures that could actually stand alone, conveying a general mood: a stark tree against a lowering autumn sky, a section of cheering bleacherites, a pattern shot of horns leaning against a rehearsal hall wall. But even in these cases it would please the future reader to know that the tree is the one on the boulevard a block from the school, the cheering was at a game that ultimately was lost, that the musical instruments were stacked during a break at the state band tournament.

"But I don't want to be that specific," says the editor. "I want to represent *generalities* in this picture." Although this sounds plausible at first, it takes little contemplation to see that this is not basically accurate. If the editor wanted just "a general picture" it would be easy to obtain one. Negatives or glossies could be pulled from the yearbook or campus newspaper file. Stock pictures of any subject imaginable can be bought from commercial houses; invariably their technical excellence will be higher and in the long run their cost will be lower. Or you could borrow photos from the company who prints your yearbook or from other staffs in your state or regional press association. There are hundreds of organizations —from your own Chamber of Commerce to the Cotton Institute to the United Nations and even the consulate of Malawa—that are happy to provide glossies absolutely free.

Yet the editor would not be happy with such art. He wants pictures taken in or around his own school, of his own classmates, and during his own year in office. Just as soon as he demands this specifically he is obviously not seeking "a general picture."

Even when the editor has been convinced of the need of identification, the photographer usually still resists. "My pictures speak for themselves," he insists. "They don't need words!" That statement, too, is inaccurate and this is easily demonstrated.

Show a photograph to a group of your classmates and ask them to write a brief statement on what it means. You will be surprised at the wide divergence of interpretation. (Be sure to use "a general picture," not one that at the moment is reenforced by specific memories only a few days old.)

The author showed a group of students a picture of a mud-spattered football player, head down and frowning deeply. What did it mean?

"The player is unhappy because his team is losing."

"He has just been hurt."

"This shows football as a brutal sport that should be abolished."

"He has just fumbled and it's his fault the game was lost."

"He is lonely because his teammates have ostra-cized him."

The truth was just the opposite. He had actually caught a fumble in the air and scooted some 70 yards for the touchdown that won the game. He was frowning because he was trying to remember the details of that play for a newspaper reporter.

What then did this uncaptioned picture accomplish? Nothing except to confuse the observer.

We think in words and therefore we communicate in words. To be true communication, a picture must be translated into words. The caption makes sure that the reader translates properly.

Some editors insist that a picture function adequately when it stirs the emotions of the beholder. There is no arguing this. Whole museums are full of paintings, especially abstract ones, that do just that.

That is art, but it is not communication. Communication is conveying the meaning of the sender exactly and precisely to the receiver. If the receiver—the reader, viewer, listener, audience— translates the message so that it means something different than intended by the sender—the writer, artist, speaker, actor—then we not only fail in transmitting information, but we are also guilty of creating misinformation.

We thus constantly come back to the truism that:

Every picture must be identified!

We expand that: Every picture must have its own identification; never attempt to identify two or more pictures with a single caption or set of cutlines. Then the reader must divide up the words and apply them to the proper art. This is a relatively difficult and confusing job, and the reader either will not do it at all or will run real dangers of making a wrong match.

Captions should be physically as close as possible to their pictures. The best place for cutlines is immediately under the picture. If placed elsewhere, it must be immediately clear to the reader which type goes with which picture.

Captions should align with at least one edge of the picture. When they do not align, the difference must be so great that the reader knows the style was achieved on purpose and is not an accident in measurement.

Captions should be written in the present tense. Maybe Susie *was* the ingenue in a class play three weeks—or three years—ago. But in the photo that instant has been frozen and she *is*—right now— accepting backstage compliments.

We have already noted in Chapter 3 that identifications should begin at the "start" of a picture, in its *primary optical area*, or *POA*, and that faces are "read" as type is read, top to bottom, left to right.

When discussion has raged and ranged, many an editor will deliver what he thinks is a knockout

All up Rolf

What goes up . . .

Captain Voas.

GYMNASTICS

A strong quartet of Captain Phil (Corky) Voas, Ron Orlick, Ray Grimaldi and Rolf Leininger were the principal point producers for Coach Paul Romeo's very successful gymnastics team. The club started strong, winning three and tieing one in its first four outings. Voas, the smallest member of the squad, proved tough to beat in floor exercises. Orkin and Leininger added to the S.U. point total in a number of events, while Grimaldi was at his best on the side horse.

92

93

"SAME-PICTURE SYNDROME" is demonstrated here. Gymnast standing on his hands, no matter what minor differences, is "same picture." One at left is good; that at right is poor photo as well as being repetitive and wastes space. Gymnasts assume so many graceful poses, cameraman should have provided editor with wide choice of pictures.

PICTURE SEQUENCE, properly chosen, becomes in effect "little movie." This series of band director is well done because of significant changes in pose and almost-cinematic continuity. Series continued onto facing page and was climaxed by quarter-page blowup of last frame.

punch to the author's logic. "It's my book, after all. Why should I have to do something just because you tell me to?"

Sure, it is the editor's book in the sense of creation and production. But, more important, it is the reader's book! An editor has the prerogative of using his own taste in making many, many decisions. But he should not misuse that prerogative by doing something that serves the reader poorly; then he perverts his school's yearbook into a mere ego trip for himself.

(The author of any book—including this one—must guard against the abuse of prerogative. And so this writer hastens to point out—yes, emphasize strongly—that no editor should do anything because this book tells him to. The admonitions passed along here are valid only if they conform to demonstrable principles. And they do. The need for picture identifications, for instance, has been proven innumerable times and without exceptions by a long, long series of research projects. The results are no whim or whimsy of an editor or a writer; they are sound, concrete, and factual.)

So, although we must decry the fallacy that "A picture is worth a thousand words", we can establish the more pertinent fact that "A picture plus a dozen words is worth 1,012 words."

Art is the most conspicuous element in a yearbook and certainly a mighty important one. Your readers are constantly exposed to the best photographic and hand art in magazines and newspapers; their taste has been highly developed and they will judge your work against professional standards; so it is essential that you do your work well.

This means taking pains . . . and taking time. *Railroading* any step in handling art—rushing it through carelessly—will mar your total handiwork irreparably. So allow plenty of time, and discipline yourself to meeting the highest standards.

"USING SAME PHOTO TWICE" weakens any layout. Here pictures of teacher at top left and lower right are almost identical in pose, distance, and angle. Addition of student in lower shot does not make this "different picture"; so much space is wasted. This is two-page spread from landscaped book.

Layout
5
... Packaging the Information

Layout, for most people, is the most fascinating part of yearbook work. There is never monotony; there is a constant challenge to ingenuity and competency; there is immediate, visible result. Even though it is a fun job, layout is mightily and vitally important.

Layout is the packaging of material within a *two-page spread.* A good layout must attract and please the reader. It is a subtle road map to guide the eye to reading everything on a spread. It enhances the communications of word and picture by blending them into a smooth, logical single unit.

Because the reader always sees two facing pages, they become a single area to him and must be designed as such. Single divider pages may seem to be an exception; but even these pages must be planned to share reader attention properly with the facing page.

Layout embraces two aspects, artistic and mechanical. A good layout is as much, and exactly, a work of art as a good painting. It combines instinctive talents with learned skills. A layout— the term is used for both products—is also a blueprint, a set of instructions to the printer. Making a good floor plan requires mechanical skills that can be learned—and might as well be learned properly.

(There are many terms for the person who does layouts. In this chapter we shall call him—or her—the *designer.* His official title on the staff may be one of many, art editor, layout man, section editor, or staffer.)

Dummies

The blueprint is called a *dummy,* and there are several varieties. The earliest is a tiny, rough sketch, a *thumbnail.* This is the designer's first attempt to put on paper a mental image he has of a possible page pattern. This can be scrawled on any old piece of paper; adequate size for a spread thumbnail is about $1\frac{1}{2} \times 2\frac{1}{2}$ inches.

The next dummy is the *rough.* This is done to the same size as the finished pages. Elements are still indicated in a sketchy way, but their size is the same as in the finished product.

The instructions that go to the printer are the *final, finished,* or *polished dummy.* (It is this sheet of paper that is often called "the layout.") Here each element is in precise size and position.

Many printers provide paper for final dummies. Usually it is marked off in 1-pica squares to make it easier for the printer to follow. If your printer doesn't have such sheets, you can buy them at an art supply store. Or you can ask the printer to print the margins—and perhaps columns—of your page on bond paper. Or you can have staff members prepare sheets by hand.

Pictures are shown in a dummy by drawing their exact outline and drawing a large X from the corners. They are identified by numbers: PHOTO #1 or ART #2. "Art" is hand art. The corresponding glossy or artwork is identified by the same number on a projecting flap: PHOTO #7, PG 12. It is necessary to designate the page number on original art because numbering begins over again for each spread, so you have scores of PHOTO #1's that must be identified by page.

Type is designated by letters: COPY A. If there are only a few lines, they are shown by sets of parallel lines. If the area is large, a simple rectangle may define it.

Headlines are lettered in. The exact area (as determined by the copyfitting methods discussed in Chapters 2 and 3) is shown. It isn't necessary that your lettering exactly fill this space; its only

"THUMBNAILS" are designer's first attempt to visualize layout. Such drawings are often smaller than those shown here. Only masses, never details, are shown in tiny projections.

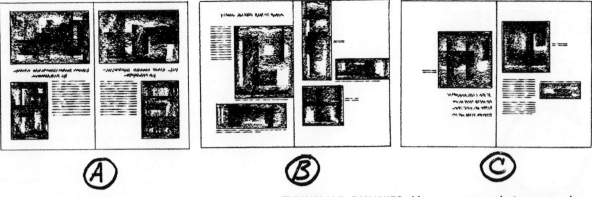

THUMBNAIL DUMMIES, like most page designs, are done in two-page spreads. A shows formally balanced pair of pages; B and C are informally or "dynamically" balanced.

job is to identify the head. Some editors like to write in the point size as well. This sometimes aids the printer, especially if there are several heads on a spread.

If you have color to use, it is wise to tint the whole area to appear in color. No matter what the color is, use a light blue or yellow pencil to show it. Write COLOR and circle it, within the area.

Any extraordinary instructions to the printer are written in margins. Be sure that instructions are written on the proper copy. Everything pertaining to the setting of type must go on the copy paper; everything concerning the placing of elements on a page must be on the dummy; platemaker's instructions must be attached to artwork.

The typesetter has nothing to do with making up a page. Nor does the platemaker. The makeup printer never sees typed copy or glossies. If instructions for one craftsman are written on material that goes to another, he may never see it. And

it's rather difficult to follow orders on a piece of paper several yards, or even miles, away.

A carbon copy should be made of every final dummy. The original may be lost en route or at the printer's—you need insurance.

Layout Specifications

There are a few constants, some of which we have already discussed, that lay ground rules for the designer.

Margins must be established in pleasing proportions. Once margins are determined, they should be as rigid as the Berlin Wall. If you vary them from page to page, the results probably will not be happy.

With the exception of folios and two-page and running heads, nothing should trespass on the

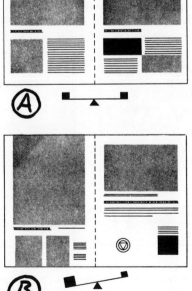

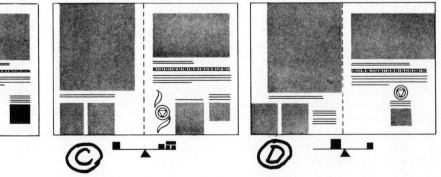

BALANCE IN LAYOUT is obtained just as on seesaw. In A, balance comes from equal typographic or optical weights equidistant from fulcrum. B leans to left because of weight of large picture. But in C, several small elements add up to enough weight to balance large picture. In D, smaller and lighter elements are moved out from fulcrum to balance large mass at left.

In no instance is there perfect balance . . . and there shouldn't be. Page or spread that "leans" a little is more pleasing to eye than one in perfect symmetrical balance . . . and thus static and dull.

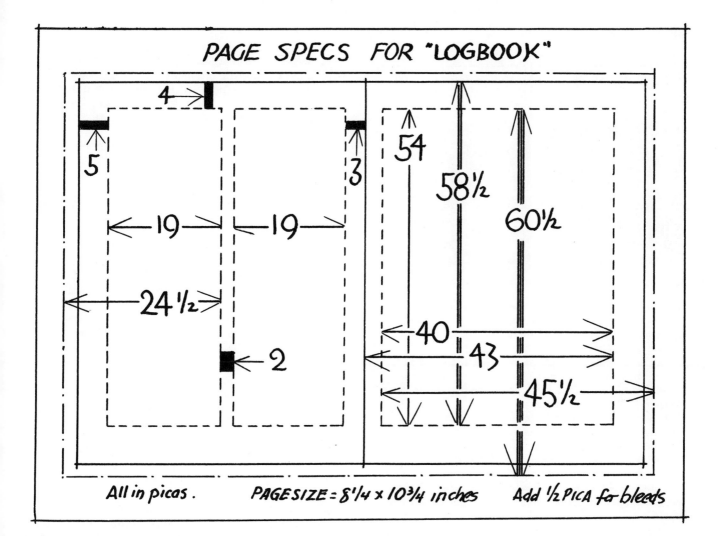

PAGE SPECS FOR "LOGBOOK"

All in picas.   PAGE SIZE = 8¼ x 10¾ inches   Add ½ PICA for bleeds

margins. We may *bleed* a picture, let it run right off a page. But nothing should project part way into a margin or float around in that space. A page need not be completely filled. But at least one element—type or picture—must define each of the four margins.

When a headline runs from one page to the next, it must extend into the gutter on each page. Otherwise the space between words at the gutter becomes greater than that between other pairs of words. This excessive space will tend to fracture the head. The headline shouldn't become lost in the fold, of course. The best result is obtained when the head extends about half the width of the gutter margin into the gutter.

Such heads must be written so there is a *word space* at the gutter. To attempt to run a single word—or even a closely linked phrase—across the gutter will destroy continuity of reading.

Each picture must have identification and that should be placed as close as possible to the art. A basic style must be adopted and adhered to. Never should a single set of cutlines identify two or more pictures.

Minimum space between pictures must be

"SPEC SHEET" shows all dimensions necessary to produce proper dummy. (Note that half pica, at least, must be added to picture to allow for bleed off page.) Chart like this should be large enough to be seen by every person working on layout. Some editors hang large one on wall; others provide smaller copies to all workers.

established. One pica is appropriate. For small pictures, such as senior portraits, the space can be as small as 4 points, an eighteenth of an inch. Such division should be an inviolate minimum; often it will be increased; there is no maximum.

Ideally, all dummying should be done after all pictures are at hand. Only when the designer knows what he has to work with can he properly display those elements in a page pattern. Unfortunately, pressures of time require that at least thumbnails often be drawn long before the picture is even taken.

When a *pre-dummy* must be used, the designer should indicate, at least roughly, what kind of picture is to be taken. It would be rather foolish to dummy in a tall, skinny picture when it must be one of fifty people in the Drama Club; a group that size can usually be posed only for a horizontal photo.

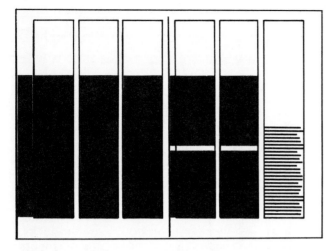

TESTING LAYOUT IDEAS may be done by cutting properly sized rectangles out of gray paper and placing them on page dummy. (Some editors even use two or more shades of gray to indicate tone of photo proposed.)

This is "oriented layout." All elements align with at least one other one. Here common axis is at top and bottom of all elements except type block (indicated by parallel lines), which orients only at bottom.

This is also called "columnar layout." Page is divided into desired number of columns. Every element begins or ends at column margin except when it bleeds off page. This layout would be more interesting if one of two identical rectangles at top of right-hand page were made taller. (Pictures should never be of exactly same size and shape.) Note that photo at lower left of left-hand page is dominant one.

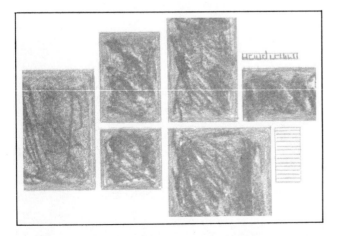

TONAL VALUE OF PHOTOS in suggested layout is indicated by crayoned rectangles drawn onto full-sized sheet. Note that this is "oriented layout." But three picures—at left of each page—are so nearly alike in shape and size that there is no dominant photo, and this layout is not nearly as pleasing to eye as it would be with that desired variety.

As a precaution against such an obvious gaffe, the designer should always do a rough sketch of each picture in a predummy, one drawn before actual pictures are available. These sketches can then be a basic guide to the cameraman when he goes out on assignment.

But though a predummy must often be used, the layout must be kept flexible enough to make changes if the final photography demands it. It would be incredibly stupid if a designer used a mediocre photo because it fit into a preconceived page pattern when a superior, but not anticipated, picture was available.

Drawing a good dummy, in any stage, is a skill that must be learned and should be practiced. The best way to learn it is to work in reverse. Take a spread from a previous yearbook or a magazine or an advertisement and draw dummies—thumbnail, rough, and final—from it. This enables you to visualize the finished product from the blueprint when you work in the normal sequence, dummy to print.

Consistency

As he draws the first dummy, the designer seeks *harmony* and *contrast*.

Each successive pair of pages must look as if they belong with all previous spreads. Much of this unity comes from well-defined and constant margins and from the use of the same typefaces. But harmony is equally dependent on an undefinable but unmistakable consistency in style.

Consistency depends on style, editorial as well as typographic. Is your book conservative, dynamic, formal, chatty? Are your photos formal or candid? Do you keep most pages well filled or are they markedly airy with white space? Are bleeds many or rare?

William Faulkner was once asked how he could keep track of all the many characters who appeared, not only in each long book, but in a whole series of books, and how he could keep the characterizations consistent.

He said: "I just know my characters so well that I'm always sure what they'll be doing in any situation." The yearbook editor must be so familiar with all details of his book that he knows instinctively whether any spread will harmonize. He must constantly reexamine the carbons of each previous spread so he can visualize the whole book as he works on a new layout.

On large books especially, several people may work on the designing job. In this case, the art editor or editor in chief must examine each layout closely to assure that harmony has been maintained.

Another method of assuring harmony is to have a *uniform tonal value* for all spreads. This means that each spread should use about as much ink as each other one. If a heavy picture is used on one spread, the designer may use two light pictures of much greater area on another. This principle is difficult to explain, but easy to see. If, as the editor checks through his dummies, he notices that some spreads look heavy or extremely light, he knows that consistency has been violated. Obviously, this tonal uniformity does not apply to contrast spreads or pages. The definite break from the basic color value is good; those pages that are almost-but-not-quite in harmony are the ones that disturb the reader.

The designer also seeks contrast. If several spreads have carried many small pictures, a full-page or two-page picture will be pleasant. If several pages have carried pictures of little interrelationship—as those of senior portraits—a picture essay or story, with several photos that are closely linked, offers needed contrast. Whenever a contrasting layout is used, it must be markedly contrasting. But way-out contrast must be used sparingly, lest it pall on the reader.

Principles of Layout

Each layout is tailor-made. Its function is to present in the most logical, interesting, and pleasing way those materials that must be shown on a spread. Because the components vary constantly, layouts must vary too. There are no stock layouts that can be taken off a shelf and put into use. There is a severe danger in copying a layout, just as is, from some other yearbook. What might have been a stunning spread in last year's *Chronicle* from Populated Area High could easily be a dull *F* in your book unless the pictures and copy you use are identical. Chances of a 100 percent duplication of material are pretty slim.

The designer can't have a handy-dandy pocket reference book listing *100 Do-It-Yourself Layouts*. He must master basic principles that do not vary; then he can apply them to constantly changing problems he confronts.

Blanket requirements for a good layout are:
1. It must be *functional*;
2. It must be *organic*;
3. It must be *invisible*.

Functional Layout

Functionalism requires that every element within a layout—or in a book—from a large picture to a single line of type, perform a useful job. If it doesn't, it should be eliminated, forthwith if not sooner. Nonfunctional elements distract the reader and weaken the design.

An organic layout, like anything organic, is a growing thing. It is a page pattern that develops logically from the materials the designer has to work with. Lines of force, for instance, will determine approximately the position of pictures. Importance of a picture determines its size. The way the eye reads out of a headline and into a copy block will influence their placement on the page and relation to each other.

Other words that are almost synonymous with organic are *logical* and *appropriate*. All elements must be so arranged that the reader can go from one to the other without having to puzzle out the path of the eye. Appropriate use of photos and type, of course, "grows" from their nature. A spread on honor societies would be different from one on basketball; if they are appropriate to the subject, they are organic.

When a designer says a layout is *invisible*, he means that it is unobtrusive; that the reader's attention is focused on the communication rather than on its arrangement. This rules out gimmicks, too-fussy decorations, and tricky arrangements that catch the eye and befuddle it.

Layout Patterns

Layout may be *formal* or *informal*. Formal page patterns are perfectly balanced. A symmetric layout will have a picture, let's say, in the top left corner and one of the same size in the right corner to balance it. Always elements will be arranged so that they would form a mirror image if the page were folded in two, vertically, horizontally, or diagonally. A *centered* layout, self-explanatory by name, also creates symmetry on a vertical axis.

Formal layouts are the easiest to do. When appropriate, they are pleasant. But they are static and dignified, too dignified most of the time, to match the content and audience of a yearbook.

Informal, or *dynamic*, layouts have movement, life, and interest. The elements are balanced, but not obviously, not by sheer mathematics.

The designer thinks of his spread as a piece of plywood. At the optical center, about 10 percent higher on the page than the mathematical center, he visualizes a pivot on which the board hangs freely. As he places each element, he visualizes it as a smaller piece of wood, nailed to the board. He arranges these "weights" to keep the board hanging almost straight. Two or more light elements balance a heavy one. A light element farther from the pivot will balance a heavier one close to the center, and so on.

There is no formula for determining the "weight of elements"; the designer must rely on his instinct and eye. The amount of ink an element deposits on the paper is the factor.

A large picture is heavier than a smaller one. One with a dark background weighs more than one in light tone.

Vertical pictures outweigh those of similar area in horizontal shape. Pictures at the top of the page are heavier than those of the same size at the bottom.

Elements at the right of the pivot will be a little heavier than those on the left; the natural reading

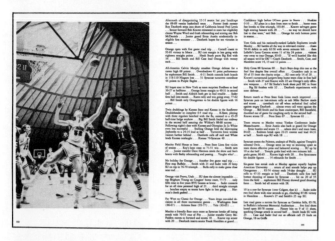

POOR LAYOUT is result of inadequate margins, lack of headline and subheads, and failure to "defend margins." Those of left-hand page are larger than those of right. Disparity between top margins is most disturbing because it is slight. Reader then feels that it is simply an error. When difference is marked, he assumes it was done on purpose.

movement of the eye tends to tip the balance a little.

Boldface type is heavier than the normal face; condensed is heavier than extended or normal.

A headline—of any type—will weigh about half as much as a photograph of the same area, as the white space surrounding, and captured by, the letters lightens the weight.

Circles, ovals, or free forms outweigh rectangles of the same area.

A good way to learn to judge weight and to check out a dummy is to cut out pieces of gray construction paper the same shape and size of the proposed photos. The designer should use three tones of gray to represent the tonal value of the art. Headlines and copyblocks in appropriate faces are cut out of magazines. These elements can then be moved around to determine the most pleasing arrangement.

It is almost impossible to make a page "hang perfectly perpendicularly." But a slight imbalance is pleasing to the eye; it contributes life and action. We don't want a page to lean so far it might fall on its face; but a little leaning is stimulating.

Reading Procedure

We have been taught to read a page starting at the top left corner and continuing to the lower right. That starting point, top left, is the *primary optical area, POA*; the bottom right is the *terminal area*. The path between the two is the *reading diagonal*. Pages that define that diagonal, even though unobtrusively, have a dynamic thrust that is interesting. The lower left and top right areas are the *fallow corners;* if we want the eye to inspect them, we must set up *optical magnets* to

lure it from the reading diagonal.

The eye rebels against going into reverse gear. It doesn't want to move upward or to the left. At the end of a line, the eye instinctively moves to the left to start the next line. To this it doesn't object. But it will not willingly go farther to the left than the start of the first line of type in the block.

This means we must have an *attention compeller* in the POA. As the eye enters a page or spread, it must find something interesting there. If the POA is weak, the eye will move to the strongest magnet on the page; anything higher or to the left of that element will not be very effective. In some instances, the eye will not go backward. At other times it will reverse its natural flow, but only reluctantly and with an irritation that detracts from reading pleasure.

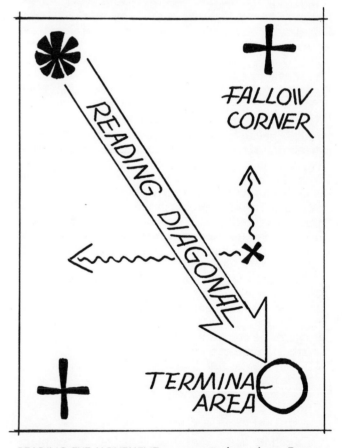

READING-EYE MOVEMENT on page is shown here. Eye enters page—or spread or any subdivision of them—in top-left corner, "primary optical area" or "POA." It instinctively moves downward and to right in "reading diagonal," toward "terminal area," for that, we all assume, is "end of page."

To lure eye into "fallow corners," designer must place "optical magnets" there. (If page is not to be totally filled, fallow corners are best left blank.)

Wavy lines indicate "reverse paths," upward and toward left, that reading eye makes reluctantly and with irritation . . . or not at all.

Understanding of this principle has coined an axiom: *"picture above type."* The strong pull of the picture may draw the eye right over the type without reading, so captions and cutlines should normally be placed under a picture. Large headlines, because their magnetism is high, may run above pictures of less pulling power. A picture bleeding at the bottom, of course, requires a caption above or at the side. These fairly unusual cases will not detract from reading pleasure.

To fill the American mind with some concept, however incomplete, of the workings of a foreign culture is a task of almost limitless depth and difficulty. It is to meet this demand that Fletcher has continued its course in French, German, Spanish, and Latin. Attitudes to which students have not formerly been exposed, words which have no clear English parallel, customs which, without understanding every nuance and implication of speech, will only be misinterpreted, were conveyed as completely as possible to the students at Fletcher, broadening and deepening their range of comprehension immeasurably. In each of these classes, knowledge was presented that will enrich these student's lives, further the communication between individuals and nations and hopefully contribute to the building of a more international point of view.

If math may be considered a language, as it was certainly intended to be by its developers, then it may also be considered foreign to many of the students at Fletcher. However, this system of symbols and equations was invented for the purpose of providing a more efficient, constructive, and truly universal means of communication than had previously existed. It incorporated and modified concepts which were formerly isolated, and produced from them a well-structured, clearly defined, and highly versatile method of expression. This language was taught on levels ranging from Business Math to Analysis I, and as students assimilated and organized its vocabulary for use in common, as well as uncommon situations, they became exposed to an entirely new area of interest and exploration.

Lower Middle: Craig Hoffman extends himself to one point on a colorful dodecahedron. *Lower Left:* In a frame of steel and wire, Nancy Cliett is surrounded by foreign sounds. *Upper Left:* Jan Porcari gets a helping hand as she adds some of the colors of France to a French class wall. *Upper Middle:* Building the Eiffel Tower, Butch Burr brings a small part of France home. *Upper Right:* Rachel Messina smiles gently while Rob Schneiker plays with the giant slide rule.

The coupling of expression

There is the University of Georgia, and there is the community of Athens, Georgia. Once the two met only for Administrative necessities. But some University students could not ignore the pressing needs of the underprivileged sector of the Athens community. Those were students who were not content simply to attend classes enveloped within an ordered, prosperous academic world. These students sought involvement with the problems of the less advantaged community surrounding the University. Thus . . .

IMPROPERLY PLACED HEADLINES are malfunctional. Placed below story, these heads draw reading eye to that area of page instead of directing it into start of article. Heads should never be to right of, or below, start of body type. (Note how face of teacher here has been lost in deep fold of gutter.)

mmunityuniversity**communiversity**

Guidance

Faced each year with the task of acquainting a new class of students to the ways of a senior high, Fletcher's Guidance Staff again proved themselves worthy of their title—guidance.

This year's faculty of Mrs. Latimer, Mr. Fay, and Mr. Packard welcomed a new member, Mrs. Torres. The counselors armed with SAT and ACT scores and college handbooks sought to help end Fletcher's educational confusion, conflicts, and indecision for another year. The counselors aided the students in adjusting courses and were the guiding hands in selecting colleges and career pursuits.

Each counselor added his own personal wealth of knowledge, varied in interest and background. These counselors, together, proved to be an invaluable source of information and they led the students in making decisions which were of profound importance to their futures.

Friendly atmospheres yield trusted advice

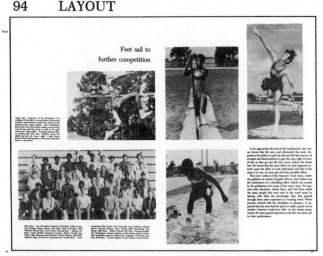

Feet sail to
further competition

READING PATH from head to start of article must be kept as short and direct as possible. Here head is properly placed above and to left of start of body type. But it is so far away from article that eye is distracted by other elements en route.

The designer must find the lines of force in each picture and place the photo so that those lines direct the eye into another picture or a block of type. You would be annoyed if you followed a large red arrow and found it directed you to a blank wall or an open field. So the reader is irritated if the arrow in a picture directs him to nothing.

"Point the picture into the page" is a valid axiom. Almost invariably, a picture looking out of the spread weakens the layout to an alarming extent.

The placement of body type must conform to the flow of the reading eye.

The path between the end of the headline and the start of the body type should be as direct and short as possible. There should be no barrier in that path. (A picture is the most common of such barriers.)

The headline should never be below or to the right of the start of the story. This explains the danger of running a head at the bottom of a page or on the right-hand page when the body type is on the left.

The path of the reading eye from one leg of type to the next should also be direct, short, and obvious. Ideally, the second column should not start higher than the first. This is not always possible to achieve, of course, but when such placement is necessary, there should be no artwork in that second column. Aligning legs of body type at their top is a good way of orienting a layout and tying together facing pages.

Especially when the copy block jumps from one page to the facing one, the intervening path should be just as short as possible.

Never place a one-column picture in a column of type and expect the reading eye to jump across

it. When the eye hits such an interruption, it instinctively will move upward and to the right to start the next column. If it does jump across the barrier to continue reading in the first column, it will do so only ineffectively and unhappily. The shorter the amount of body type below such a barrier, the greater the danger that it will not be read at all.

Reading irritations may be—usually are—minor; often the reader is not even consciously aware of them. It is not fatal if a violation occurs once in a while, but the accumulation becomes major. The difference between superiority and mediocrity is usually dependent on how well the staff masters details.

Dominant Elements

One element on a page must very obviously be the most important and dominate the layout. Pictures are best arranged on the *hen-and-chick* principle, one large photo around which smaller ones are placed. The dominant picture should be at least 50 percent "heavier" and larger than the next largest.

A layout of a group of pictures all the same shape and size is not very exciting. Thus, on the senior portrait page, where pictures must be all alike, the designer faces an acute problem.

Such portraits must be arranged alphabetically for convenience of the reader. If they are placed to make a neat rectangle, there will be occasions when a picture will be forced to face off the page. (It is to minimize this that the photographer is instructed not to make full profile portraits.) This problem can be solved by arranging portraits in an irregular pattern; then the distracting picture can be moved to the start of the next line where it will face into the page. Varying the length of rows also

"DOMINANT PICTURE" at lower left acts as "hen" to carry out designer's basic "hen-and-chick principle." Open area between two top pictures weakens layout here, and it would be better if top-left photo were moved toward center of spread.

A few snowflakes fell in pairs on the winter days. Inside and out paths and minds branched out in different directions. There was a feeling of joy at either the cold wetness of the snow or the preoccupation of one's mind on his work.

Liz Fabry.

Leslie Palanker.

Snow whispering down
all day long
Earth has vanished
leaving only sky.
Joso

Fred Garver, the great Garbo.

The Snow family.

Being absorbed.

Playing in the first snowstorm.

6

7

prevents monotony in page patterns. This technique requires more space for the senior section, but the result is worth the investment of space.

Monotony can also be avoided by occasionally leaving a blank space within a row of portraits; or, in that space, running the school seal, a theme drawing, or just a decorative piece of hand art. This technique enables shifting a portrait that faces the wrong way. The same device is pleasant when used on many, or all, such pages. But only one such decorative element should be used on each page.

Another device, which doesn't use extra space, is to run the identification of a single portrait per page above, rather than under, the picture. This breaks the tedious series of straight lines of pictures.

The hen-and-chick principle can be used on portrait pages by using atmosphere or record shots, or photo stories, as the "hen" on these pages. Or faculty portraits, larger than those of students, may run on these pages. This doesn't require more space because this is material that would be run anyway.

Never should student portraits, even of class

"DOMINANT PICTURE" acts as nucleus for well-designed page pattern. Here it is one at lower right. Dominant one must be at least 50 percent larger than next-larger photo. Picture in light tone, as here, must be even greater in area.

Star indicates point where two lower pictures miss alignment by just one pica. Had they been properly lined up, this would be excellent example of oriented layout.

officers, be run in larger sizes on portrait pages. Each student must be given exactly the same treatment as all others.

The designer should not "use the same picture" more than once. This doesn't mean the same photograph, of course; the "picture" may be the same in several "photographs." If one shot is of a student looking through a biology microscope, all other pictures of microscope peerers will be duplicative.

Pictures of groups should be so cropped and scaled that all head sizes on a spread are approximately the same. The good designer would not use the six-man debating team in a half-page photo alongside the sixty-member Future Teachers group. The effect would be of Gulliver and the Lilliputians.

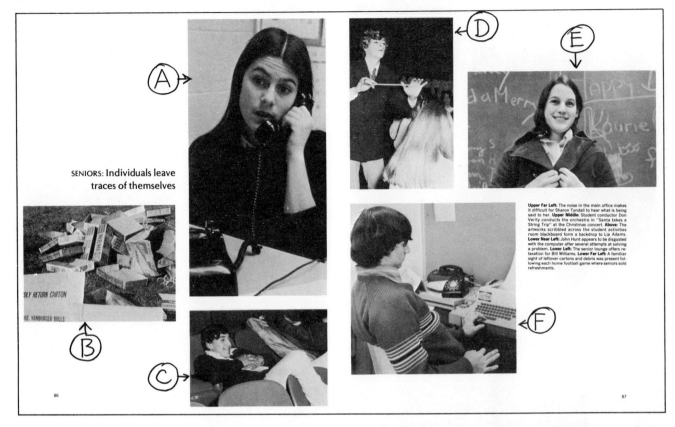

SENIORS: Individuals leave traces of themselves

Upper Far Left: The noise in the main office makes it difficult for Sharon Tyndall to hear what is being said to her. Upper Middle: Student conductor Don Verity conducts the orchestra in "Santa takes a String Trip" at the Christmas concert. Above: The artworks scribbled across the student activities room blackboard form a backdrop to Lia Adams. Lower Near Left: John Hunt appears to be disgusted with the computer after several attempts at solving a problem. Lower Left: The senior lounge offers relaxation for Bill Williams. Lower Far Left: A familiar sight of leftover cartons and debris was present following each home football game where seniors sold refreshments.

86

87

Oriented Layouts

The most pleasing layouts are those done in *oriented patterns*. This princple is also called the *buddy system* or the *no-orphan* technique.

By this technique, every element is aligned—vertically most of the time, but also horizontally—with at least one other. Each element is buddied-up with at least one other, and so none stands all by itself; there are no orphans.

Alignment may be flush left, flush right, centered, or on either side of a line drawn along the end of a picture or type block or the end of a headline; so the left margins of two pictures may line up or the left edge of one on the right margin of the other.

Although most *orientation* is on the edges of photos, it can be done on strong lines within a photo. With a head-on picture of your school, for instance, you might align another element on the edge of a wall instead of that of the photo.

Always, orientation must be obvious. The more buddying-up within a layout, the more cohesive the composition and the more pleasing to the eye. Each dummy should be checked for strong orientation before it is sent to the printer.

Although each margin of the type page must be defined by at least one element, that page need not be completely filled as, for instance, the pages of this book are. An irregular page silhouette is pleasant, and white space—called *fresh air* by the

"ORIENTED LAYOUT" is demonstrated by this spread. Picture A shares vertical axis with C and horizontal one with D.

Pictures D and F align vertically and D and E line up at bottom. Headline aligns at right with B, copy block at top with F.

If photo B were moved upward to align with top of C or bottom of A, orientation would be perfect. Photo A is dominant picture.

When oriented layout is concentrated into center of spread, it is also called "mosaic layout." Term should not be confused with "mosaic cropping" of photograph.

typographer—is as pleasant in a book page as in a classroom.

White space should be placed on the outside of a layout, to create that distinctive outline. White space within a layout—*trapped space*—makes the composition disintegrate. The hole-in-the-doughnut effect can make the layout look as if it were flying apart by centrifugal force.

Jumping the Gutter

The yearbook is designed as a series of two-page spreads. Each pair must join into an integral unit. The designer must overcome the divisive effect of the white strip that runs down the gutter and breaks the spread in two.

Jumping the gutter is a constant problem. The designer must always look for ways to tie the pages together.

The most obvious way is to run a headline or

LOST IN GUTTER sounds like title of Victorian melodrama. Actually it is typographic mishap, but just as sad. Here deep fold of gutter has completely swallowed face of pretty (you have to take my word for it!) girl and of cowboy-hatted principal.

If photos must run across gutter, care must be taken that no important detail falls within two picas on either side of center of spread.

picture across the gutter. But this creates a new set of problems.

Facing pages of a spread are not printed side by side, except at the center of each signature. In some books, facing pages may even be on different sheets of paper. If a page is just a trifle off on the margin—on the press or, more often, the folder— elements that are supposed to align may be off enough to break the horizontal line. If one page is a trifle high and the other just a bit low, the compounding can throw alignment badly off.

Possibilities of misalignment are slight, less than 10 percent. But the able staff won't risk even this.

To avoid the danger, heads can be written so that a large type is used on the left page and a smaller one on the right. If the top of the smaller type is aligned with the bottom of the larger, misalignment will not be so obvious.

Spreading a picture across the gutter ties the two pages together but runs the same risk in aligning. A greater danger, however, is that a portion of the picture may be hidden in the binding. If this is an essential portion, the effect is most distressing.

Bleeds

Bleeding pictures is a good technique. As the photo breaks out of the basic rectangle of the type area, it expands not only that area but the whole page.

When a picture is to *bleed*, it must be made 1 pica larger than it will appear in print. If a picture is dummied to bleed off the left margin, and it will be 24 × 30 picas on the printed page, it must be marked to be made 25 picas wide. If the same picture is also to bleed off the bottom, a pica must be added to its height, so it would be marked for 25 × 31. If it bleeds both top and bottom, it must be marked 2 picas taller than the page height.

This scaling must be done after cropping, of course, just as if there were no bleed.

This extra size is required because bleeds are made by printing the picture on a larger sheet of paper, then trimming it—right through the picture—to proper size. It is impossible to print a picture so that it hits precisely on the edge of the sheet.

Pictures that bleed to the gutter do not require this extra allowance for trimming because there the page is just folded, not cut. Occasionally you may notice that the folding has not been precise. There may be a sliver of white at the gutter, or the picture may intrude a trifle on the page that faced

WINTER WEEKEND, The Class of 70 class T.G.I.F. . . . The Fifth Dimension at the War Memorial . . . Big Ski-Dance of snow and with luck the sculptures hands and feet in the below zero, wonc

WINTER comes to

it during printing but which usually will not be a facing one in the finished book. Thus the reader will see, at the gutter of the other page, a strip of halftone for which there is no apparent reason; it looks like a streak of dirt.

Obviously, two pictures should not bleed from opposite pages into the gutter at the same point. They will, in effect, become just a single picture and will confuse the reader.

Good designers carry this one step further; they will never bleed two pictures to the gutter, either on the same or facing pages.

Gutter bleeds are usually not very effective. There is no expanding effect; the fold stops the enlarging motion. All the designer gains is the little extra space of the margin.

Alignment of elements on opposite pages by the orientation system ties the spread together. Even if there is misalignment on the folder, the elements will be far enough apart so the wavering of the horizon is not apparent.

The same added color on both pages also acts as a tie to unify the spread.

If headline and pictures are obviously related, on a baseball spread, for instance, facing pages can be tied together by using only pictures (with

"BLEEDS" OFF PAGE are most effective at outside margin rather than to gutter. Here lower right photo expands as it bleeds off bottom and seems to increase size of entire spread. Expanding effect of picture at left center is stopped by gutter. (This is "picture essay" and small block of body type is adequate.)

idents, of course) on one page and only type on the facing one. In this case, the picture page should be on the left, lest it draw the eye away from the type page of lesser optical magnetism.

Pictures with strong lines of force tend to tie the spread together when they face into the gutter. A single block of type, toward which strong arrows point from both sides, is a good link between pages.

When copy reads from one page to the other, instead of as self-contained blocks on each page, the eye will instinctively jump the gutter to continue reading; so copy on the first page should end within a paragraph instead of at the widow. This link is an unobtrusive one and must be reenforced with a typographic bond.

Consistency in general typographic and photographic style is a strong tie between facing pages, as it is among all pages.

NONFUNCTIONAL ELEMENTS include distracting backgrounds such as these. It would be better to leave background plain and blow up photos to larger images.

Ornaments

Stress on functionalism leads many staffs to shun the use of *ornaments*, hand art or typographic. But ornaments can be functional. You can use them to guide the eye through a spread, to break monotonous picture patterns (as we've already noted in the use of the school seal on the senior portrait pages), or to please the reader's eye . . . as the Pennsylvania Dutch say: "Just for pretty."

Before any ornament is used, the designer must ask: "Does this serve a useful purpose?" Unless it is perfectly obvious that the answer is yes, don't use the ornament.

Some ornamentation is consistently nonfunctional.

Periodically, a fad revives the 1930 technique of using large blocks of black or gray. This is a waste of space. It would be much better to enlarge the pictures. The use of strips of black or gray— wide or narrow—"to tie the composition together" is just a public admission that the designer has failed to achieve a good page pattern with the basic elements.

Borders around a page are useless and constrictive. They cut down the size of the page, obviously preclude bleeds, fragment the spread, distract the eye.

Often a designer will use an overall background for a page. This may be a repetitive pattern such as a favorite one of autumn leaves. Or it may be of a familiar texture such as the leather of a football. Sometimes it is a *ghosted* photograph, one printed very lightly. Elements may be pasted—or overprinted—directly onto the background or they may be placed in internal mortices. Happy results from this technique are practically nonexistent.

Any background, no matter how pleasant or unobtrusive, affords less contrast to black type than white paper would. This diminution of contrast lowers legibility of type. Bolder backgrounds

—even if type is morticed in—compete with the type or pictures for reader attention.

In many cases, the designer cannot make photos as large as they might otherwise be—or ought to be—because the design of the background will then be lost.

The most distracting background is the solid black. Type reversed onto such background—to appear as white—is difficult to read, and pictures are overpowered. Good use of all-black background is rare.

Hand art used to frame halftones usually just clutters up the page. The best frame for a photo is white space.

Layout Procedures

Laying out a good spread is as definitely a creative process as composing a melody. It would be presumptuous to tell a composer, step by step, how to create . . . or to tell a designer. One thing is sure, however: You can't sit around waiting for the Muse to beam the light of inspiration on you. The cliché about 1 percent inspiration and 99 percent perspiration applies to yearbook layout as much as to the inventions of Thomas Edison, who first formulated the recipe. Deadlines will not wait on inspiration; so we might as well learn to apply sweat.

These steps are necessary to do a layout:
1. Draw the margins of the page.
2. Inspect all pictures.
3. Decide which will be the dominant one.
4. Determine the lines of force within each picture.
5. Crop and scale each picture.
6. Place them so that lines of force direct the eye logically.
7. Place captions and/or idents.
8. Place the headline and/or running heads.
9. Place the body type block.
10. Check that every element is well oriented.
11. Check especially those pages immediately before the spread (and those right after, if they have been prepared out of order) to make sure that this spread is harmonious with all others.
12. Tell the copy editor how much type can go on the spread.

Naturally, you will be applying all the principles of good layout that we have discussed in this chapter.

To determine whether a layout is pleasing, the editor must trust his own eye and taste. Once he has followed basic principles, the final approval depends on whether the layout "looks right" to him. As he makes a last check, the editor should look for those common errors that mar many yearbook pages. A list of strong DON'TS include:

1. Don't crowd pages. Maintain margins and give breathing room to pix and type.
2. Don't jumble pages. Arrange every element so that it can be read in logical sequence and doesn't suffer from competition of adjoining ones.
3. Don't get too gimmicky. "Clever" layouts don't wear well.
4. Don't let the art background overpower the communicative elements.
5. Don't use any element—especially art—unless it serves a useful function.
6. Don't tilt elements on a page or the whole page. Don't run a page sideways. It is better to run an extremely wide picture across the gutter rather than sideways on a page.
7. Don't use collages. Don't use montages.
8. Don't leave blank pages for autographs. They're too expensive to use for writing paper and usually give the impression that the staff was unable to fill them with interesting material. Besides, most students prefer to sign their name on the page with their picture.

NONFUNCTIONAL ELEMENTS hamper easy communication. Reading is made difficult here by wavy lines below *Cross Country*, and "reversed type" (white on black) is always more difficult to read than positive image.

On *Activities* page, two borders at bottom add nothing of value. On all four pages, artwork is superfluous, and wide variety of headletters is confusing. But though all these nonfunctional elements were included, one essential—identification of photos—was left out!

Advertising

Advertising is an important part of a yearbook. It must be properly displayed to attain maximum readership so that the advertiser obtains results. Well-designed ads are pleasant to the reader and certainly do not "intrude" on editorial matter nor detract from the reader's pleasure.

All-ad pages (unless it's a full-page ad, of course) are not as useful to the advertiser as those pages in which only about half is used for editorial copy. Ads should be placed at the bottom of the page. If a *half-pyramid pattern* is formed by ads,

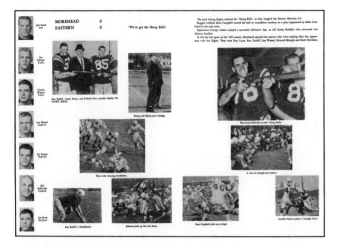

"POORLY WOVEN" PAGES create "trapped space" in spread below. Top margin is far too scanty; lines of force carry eye off page. Bleeding portraits—always dangerous and especially in small sizes as here—results in uncomfortable cropping.

On *Cheerleaders* page, there is no discernible pattern in placement of pictures. "Mortice" of center picture has no purpose and is unattractive. Each cheerleader has at least one foot amputated at ankle.

the slope should be as gradual as possible and—on any page—to the right. There must be a strong editorial attention compeller in the POA of ad pages.

Title Pages

The first page of the book proper is a *singleton*. It faces the blank end paper, which is never printed on this reverse side. So the *title page* is one that is not designed in a spread—the other is the last page.

Some staffs prefer a spread for the title page; then Page 1 becomes the *half-title* page, which carries only the name of the book. Conventionally there is no ornamentation. A growing variation is to run only a small art element, without type, on the half-title page. This may be a hint of the theme, the seal or emblem of the school or yearbook.

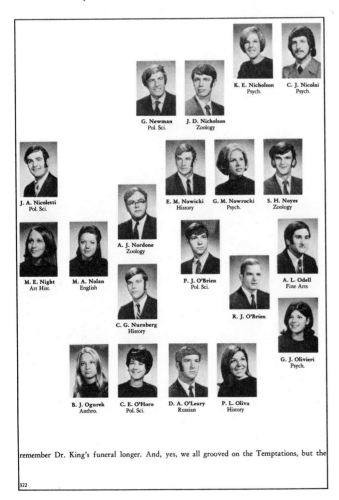

SENIORS PAGE "falls apart," because there is no obvious pattern for placement of pictures. Two areas of trapped space further weaken layout.

The full-title page carries the name of the book and school and the year. Sometimes the names of the full staff or those of the editor in chief and business manager are included.

There is a rapidly growing trend to use the full *masthead*, listing every staffer, at the very end of the book. This enables a stronger and simpler design on the title page.

If only the top student executives' names are carried on the title page, they are repeated in the full masthead.

A common fault is to make the editor's name too large, especially when it appears alone. We all know that the editor's job has been an arduous one and deserves public recognition. But modesty is always a commendable virtue and this is especially true on the title page.

The title page usually begins development of the theme by its art work. It is obvious that the art must be of the highest caliber; first impressions are most important. But the title page may be entirely typographic, leaving the theme keynote for the following pages.

Design of the title page follows the principles we have been discussing in this chapter. The page should be simple. The type should be that used on divider pages; it must be appropriate to the theme as well as to the general character of the book. Black Letter would be perfect for a King Arthur theme, but not for one on astronauts. If the general tone of the book is light and airy, with generous white space, a heavy Gothic type would be incongruous.

Elements should be combined as much as possible so that the designer has only two or three masses to work with. This will avoid the "busy" appearance of many scattered elements.

The name of the book and the date can run close together to become a single element. Artwork can tie into the name. The date might be combined with the school and city name. If the masthead runs on this page, names should be grouped tightly so they become a single block. As on any page, one element must definitely be the dominant one. Use of the buddy system is essential.

Because the amount of ink on the title page is relatively less than on most other pages, there is a tendency to use ornamentation—especially rules and borders—to fill space. Avoid the temptation. Just make sure that the elements are not too widely separated and that there is no trapped white space. Look at the title page of any well-designed novel or textbook and see how white space is used there.

Sometimes in avant-garde books several pages of photographs, suggesting the theme, appear before the title page. Effectiveness of this technique depends on the theme and how well the photos suggest it. In one successful treatment, the book had BUILDING as its theme. On opening pages, pictures of cranes, heavy equipment, and men at work made it unmistakable that building was

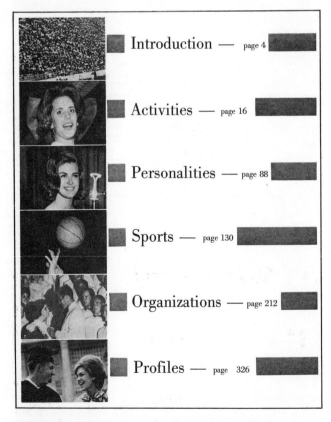

TABLE OF CONTENTS is well displayed and illustrated with art. But full page of any yearbook—especially one of less than 200 pages—is extravagant space to devote to this table . . . if it is needed at all.

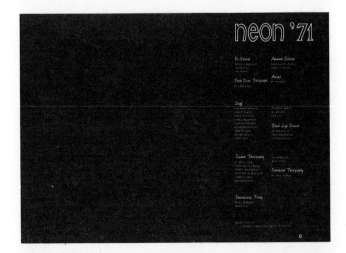

"MASTHEAD" should list complete staff, and editor's name should be unobtrusive, lest reader brand him egomaniac. This masthead, in landscaped book, is proper in size although small letters are difficult to read in reverse. Name and place of school, omitted here, are essential.

going on. The cover was a portion of a blueprint. Strips of blueprints lent color to the opening pages and reenforced the theme. The reader found the atmosphere shots interesting and a logical introduction to the title page with its big heading, BUILDING THE UNIVERSITY.

Many themes do not lend themselves to such simple pictorial statement, and so this technique should be used only rarely. Body type should not run before the title page; this is so radical a departure from the conventional book that the reader would be disturbed.

Divider Pages

Divider pages introduce major sections of the yearbook. In most instances these are an integral part of the book; sometimes dividers are printed on heavier paper, which may be in color or have a marked texture.

If the divider is a single sheet of paper, it must be *tipped in* to the book, fastened by an adhesive. This adds to production cost. Customarily, only the front of a tipped-in sheet is printed.

If the divider consists of four pages, it is sewn into the book. It must then be placed at the center-fold of a signature or between signatures and so its position is rigidly defined. This means that space must be, in some instances, stolen from a section and used in another that may not need it as much as the first.

Use of *inserted dividers* (those of different paper) should be discussed with the printer at the earliest planning stages. In most instances the extra cost is not warranted.

The divider is a major element in developing the theme. Its treatment must be appropriate to the theme and to the section and harmonious with the total book. There must be a strong family resemblance among all dividers. Usually the divider will contrast markedly with other pages in the book, especially the facing one, to make it easy for the reader to find. But the contrast must be appropriate; the divider must tie integrally into the book.

The same typeface used on the title page should be used on each divider. The size will probably be smaller than that on the title page but should be the same on all dividers.

There must be identical treatment of divider-page copy, in length and grammatical style. Suppose your theme is OUR AIMS, and the first divider, for academics, says "To Seek Knowledge." Then each succeeding divider must carry an infinitive phrase. If the label is merely ACADEMICS, each other divider should carry just a single noun.

Sometimes a *blurb*, a short paragraph of explanatory copy, accompanies the divider title. Then each divider must have a blurb, written in the same style, set in the same type and occupying the same number of lines. Don't write one blurb in

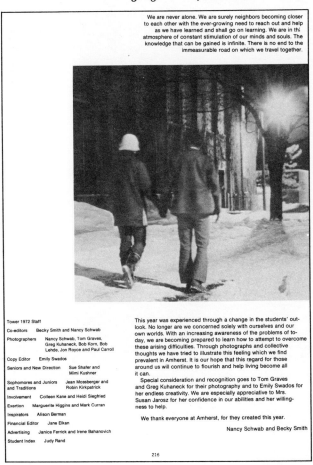

We are never alone. We are surely neighbors becoming closer to each other with the ever-growing need to reach out and help as we have learned and shall go on learning. We are in this atmosphere of constant stimulation of our minds and souls. The knowledge that can be gained is infinite. There is no end to the immeasurable road on which we travel together.

Tower 1972 Staff

Co-editors   Becky Smith and Nancy Schwab
Photographers   Nancy Schwab, Tom Graves,
                  Greg Kuhaneck, Bob Korn, Bob
                  Lehde, Jon Royce and Paul Carroll
Copy Editor   Emily Swados
Seniors and New Direction   Sue Shafer and
                            Mimi Kushner
Sophomores and Juniors   Jean Mossberger and
and Traditions   Robin Kirkpatrick
Involvement   Colleen Kane and Heidi Siegfried
Exertion   Marguerite Higgins and Mark Curran
Inspirators   Alison Berman
Financial Editor Jane Elkan
Advertising   Janice Ferrick and Irene Bahanovich
Student Index   Judy Rand

This year was experienced through a change in the students' outlook. No longer are we concerned solely with ourselves and our own worlds. With an increasing awareness of the problems of today, we are becoming prepared to learn how to attempt to overcome these arising difficulties. Through photographs and collective thoughts we have tried to illustrate this feeling which we find prevalent in Amherst. It is our hope that this regard for those around us will continue to flourish and help living become all it can.

Special consideration and recognition goes to Tom Graves and Greg Kuhaneck for their photography and to Emily Swados for her endless creativity. We are especially appreciative to Mrs. Susan Jarosz for her confidence in our abilities and her willingness to help.

We thank everyone at Amherst, for they created this year.

Nancy Schwab and Becky Smith

216

"MASTHEAD" is last page of this book. It is combined with final development of theme and editor's personal thank-you's. Masthead may be at either beginning or end of book. Often it is opposite title page or even part of it. New trend is to print masthead on "end papers."

orotund style, and another in wry, humorous, or staccato style.

Each typographic element should appear in the same relative position on each divider. The title, for instance, would be 15 picas from the bottom and 23 picas from the left margin on every page.

Whether hand or photographic, artwork on dividers must be strong. Anything less than superior quality should be rejected. The same art technique must be used on each divider page. *High key* photography—light subjects on a light background—should not be mixed with low key shots, dark and moody ones. Formal and candid posing should not be mixed. If most dividers have symbolic art, don't let one use specific pictures.

In hand art, do not mix media. Use crayon work on each divider, or pen-and-ink sketches or woodblocks. But never use more than one technique.

Divider pages are analogous to the titles that introduce a television show and each segment following commercials. Note how consistency is maintained there.

Well, we've been so many places
they tend to blend;
lost and long forgotten
are the words of memory
in time—
gone is gone
as best we can remember.
We can laugh again.

Editors: Susan Cliett, Joe Gill, and Debbie Long; Staff: Sylvia Baldwin, John Brooks, David Brown, Miles Dean, Tommy DePryscker, Ted Doss, Rochelle Gray, Denise Haney, Dana Keasler, Lori King, Jim Moses, Patty Parman, Sharon Peach, Skipper Scott, Donna Self, Patty Stanton, NeeCee Thomason, Frances Ulmer, Sarah Werner, Gail Williams, Teresa Wright; Sponsors: Miss Mary Hinkle and Miss Lucia Warren.

The single divider is designed as a self-contained composition that follows all basic design principles. Only then is the facing editorial page designed. Some editors use only type on the facing page. If art is used, it must be unobtrusive to avoid competition with the divider. Elements on the facing page should be oriented, on each other as well as on elements or lines of force in the divider.

Full-bleed photographs are effective for dividers. This usually requires *surprinting, overprinting of type.* This type should appear in the same position on each divider. Yet it cannot run over a broken, confusing background. Photos should be taken so that area for the type is in a solid tonal value. Never can important detail be included there. If the photo itself doesn't afford a solid area on which the type must run, such a solid must be created by *dodging* or *burning-in* in the darkroom when the glossy is made, or by *airbrushing* or *retouching* on the glossy.

With a four-page inserted divider, the first page usually carries the name of the section and little or no art. Second and third pages are then heavy on art that must tie the theme to the section. The fourth page may be theme material or it may become a typical page of the book proper and become a spread with the facing page of regular book paper.

Simplicity, as always, is the key to good divider

END-PAPER masthead uses posterization of photo and extra color, yellow, to accentuate black image.

design, and here, the editor must resist temptation to get cute or gimmicky.

Subdividers

Subdividers are used—or at least are necessary —only in large books, those with more than 300 pages. They introduce subdivisions such as FOOTBALL, BASKETBALL, TRACK, etc., within the SPORTS section or HONORARY, ACADEMIC or SOCIAL within the ORGANIZATIONS section.

Subdividers are single pages and are done in the same treatment as dividers. Subdivisions can also be identified by a *logotype,* a small type and/or pictorial device that occupies only part of the conventional copy page. These are a waste of space, however; the page itself ought to indicate the nature of the material in that subsection.

The subdivider can be effective as a vertical third- or half-page on the outside margin. If this is done, there is temptation to run type vertically, too. Under no circumstances should this be done. Smaller type must be used so that it can run horizontally.

Table of Contents

The need for a yearbook *table of contents* page has been challenged in Chapter 1. But if the staff decides on one, it must be handled organically. It conventionally appears just after the title page, but in yearbooks is often presented on the title page.

A common error in table of contents pages is excessive spacing between the few necessary lines of type. Type should be concentrated into a cohesive block. Its placement depends on accompanying art work.

As interesting technique is to run one of the oustanding photos from each section alongside the appropriate listing in the table. These pictures should help develop the theme as must all art on this page.

If the table runs on the title page, it should be as a block that unobtrusively ties into the page pattern.

Customarily, the section title in the table is connected to the page number with *leaders,* a row of periods or dashes. Periods are most common in book work. Leaders are required if the space between the title and page number is longer than four times the point size of the type. Thus, if 10 point is used, the gap should be no longer than 40 points, about 3½ picas, without leaders.

Index Pages

The value of an *index* is debatable. If one is used, it should be set in agate, 5½ point type, to

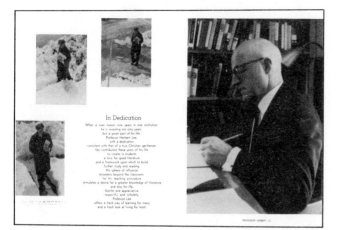

In Dedication

When a man invests nine years in one institution
he is investing not only years,
but a great part of his life.
Professor Herbert Lee,
with a dedication
consistent with that of a true Christian gentleman,
has contributed these years of his life
to create in students
a love for good literature
and a framework upon which to build
further study and reading.
His sphere of influence
broadens beyond the classroom
for his teaching procedure
stimulates a desire for a greater knowledge of literature
and also for life.
Gentle and appreciative,
respectful and scholarly,
Professor Lee
offers a fresh way of learning for many
and a fresh look at living for most.

PROFESSOR HERBERT LEE

THE DEDICATION must be genuine and graceful. It is best written by a staffer who has deep respect and affection for person thus honored. Often dedication comes near or at end of book instead of at beginning.

conserve space. It is set in three or four columns per page. The gap between type and page number should be no longer than about 2½ picas unless leaders are used.

The letter identifying each alphabetical group should be approximately 14 points.

Sans Serif has the highest legibility in agate size and should be chosen for the index no matter what body type is used elsewhere.

Index pages are exceptionally dull and should be enlivened with art. This is a good place to run a picture story or essay. The index runs at the end of the book.

Acknowledgments

A favorite method presenting the editor's personal greetings and thanks is to type a letter on the yearbook's own letterhead and reproduce it as a line cut. If this is done, a fresh ribbon should be used, and the typing done by an expert typist.

The Printer's Package

All the material for a page should be sent to the printer in a large individual envelope. (Some printers prefer the whole spread in a single package.) The name of the yearbook and the page number should be written in the top right corner of the longer dimension (as where a stamp goes on a letter). This makes for easy filing.

Inside are the page or spread dummy, text, and headline copy (on separate sheets of paper) and all artwork, hand or photo.

Each piece of copy—text, art, and the dummy—must have the name of the yearbook on it. A rubber stamp is ideal for this. Used with red ink, it is a conspicuous *flag* that indicates that the copy has been inspected by the editor; only he should use the stamp.

Many yearbook printers insist that the adviser

sign or initial every piece of copy. This is to forestall any attempt by some practical joker to sneak in unauthorized material.

As the editor inspects the package, he has a checklist that he follows meticulously.

1. Is the dummy adequate? Are all elements indicated and are special instructions clear? Is the layout functional, organic and invisible? Is it harmonious with all other spreads in the book?

2. Are all pages properly numbered (even if the number will not appear in print because of a bleed photo)? The editor checks off each page on his progress chart and/or page list. Any printer can tell you about staffs that wound up with two Page 37's or no Page 132 or with more or less pages than the book was supposed to contain.

3. Is all artwork included? The editor lays each photo or drawing on the layout to make sure. Then he checks cropping on each photo and the instruction tab. The photo that the dummy shows as 23 picas wide had surely better be marked for reduction to 23 picas! Special instructions—as for silhouetting, surprinting, etc.—must be complete and clear. The editor will make a tiny red checkmark on the dummy as each piece of art has been found adequate.

COPY CONTROL is charted in booklet of which this is spread for one 16-page signature. As pages are completed, numbers are noted in lower-right corner. Some printers prefer that complete signature be sent in; others will accept two-page spreads as staff completes them, but printing cannot start till sig is complete.

Page numbers are printed in tan (shown as gray here) and red (shown as black). All those numbered in one color are printed on one side of the same sheet of paper. If a second color is available, it can be used on any one of the eight pages at no extra cost.

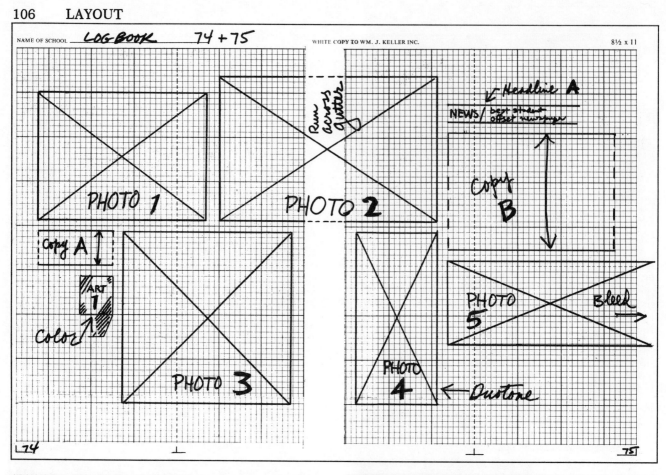

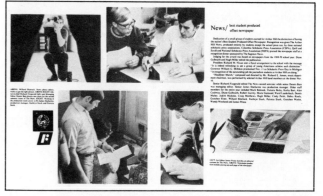

"DUMMY" (OR PAGE "LAYOUT") is always prepared in two-page spreads. Dummy above directed printer in producing spread below. Note that here pictures are numbered and copy blocks designated by letters. Such designation styles may be reversed, of course, as long as they remain consistent throughout book.

Note that *Photo 2* runs across gutter and thus is larger on dummy than in actual book because white space between pages of dummy is not part of printed page.

Area of headline is shown in actual size on dummy. Lettering on dummy may be any size, however; its function is merely one of identification at this point. Information such as use of color for *Art 1* and *Photo 4* is written in open area so it will not be overlooked. (*Art* designates hand art.) Bleeds are indicated by arrow as for *Photo 5*.

ADVERTISING DUMMY combines layout and copy of individual ads and of whole page. Some printers ask for separate copy sheets for advertising as for regular editorial pages. If typefaces and sizes are not specified, printer will use his own judgment, which, in most cases, will more than satisfy staff and advertiser.

ADVERTISING COMBINATION DUMMY AND COPY SHEET (Size 9 x 12)

All advertising must be typewritten complete, on these sheets

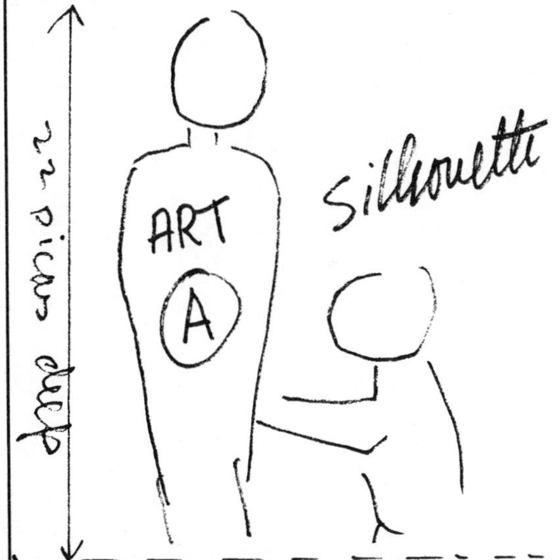

22 picas deep
ART
A
Sillouette

Jack Smithers gets fitted for the
Prom by Mr. William Seyfert at the

36 Onyx flush right Top Hat Shop

18 Spartan Italic Northwood Shopping Plaza

The finest in formal wear for sale
or rent

10 pt Tempo bold 20 picas

It's the real thing

Coke

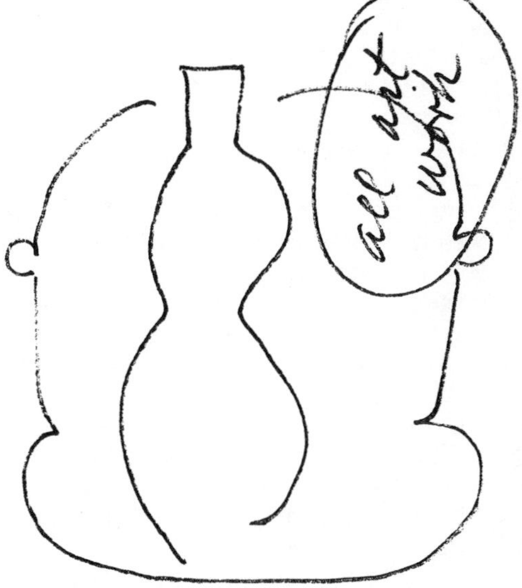

all art work

We L I K E
Northwest students at
Bill's Sunoco Service
and our service shows it!

36 Tempo Bold flush left

Come on in, like Jan Smith and
Bill McIntyre (below) who are
getting that friendly Bill's service

14 Tempo Medium 20 picas

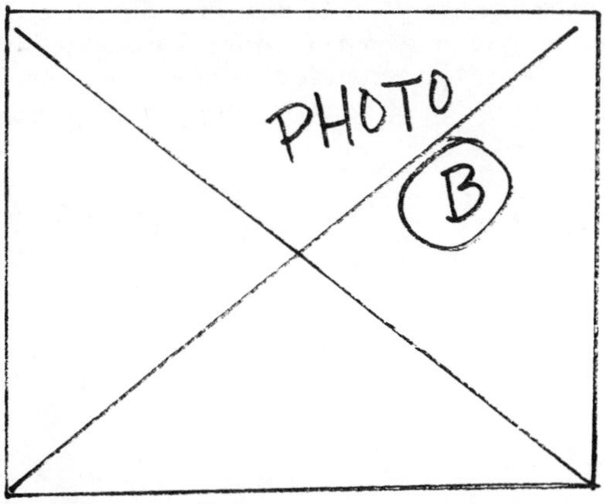

PHOTO
B

Central Avenue at 29th Street

May your four years
at Northwest High
be the beginning of a long
and happy career in the big world!*

18 Bodoni Bold set line for line flush left

Congratulations from ← 48 Bod Extra Bold Italic
N-Air Charter, Inc. ← 60 Bodoni Ex Bold flush RIGHT

*We make it smaller.

18 Bodoni Bold Italic

WM. J. KELLER INC.
33 Clarence Avenue
Buffalo 15, N. Y.

Form 36C

4. Is all caption and identification material included? As each of the accompanying copy for each picture is checked, a red x is marked on the dummy.

5. Are all headlines included? Check the dummy as each head is accounted for. Although the editor need not count characters in a head (the managing editor has long since done that), he will be able to detect an obviously long head just by looking at it. If there is doubt, he will actually count off the head copy.

6. Is all the text copy included? Again, just by looking at the dummy, the editor will be able to tell if there is a marked discrepancy between copy space allotted to it.

Although he knows that the copy editor and managing editors have copyread text matter with extreme care, the editor in chief will read through the list of names and make a final check of those that have more than one spelling: Mary Ann, Mary Anne, Marian, Marianne, Mariann, Mari Ann; Frederick, Frederic; John, Jon, etc.

7. Now he inspects the dummy to see that every element has been checked off as present.

8. Finally, he stamps the book name on each piece of copy and personally puts it into the envelope and seals it.

Layout is one of the most fascinating aspects of yearbook work. Although it is not as important as good content in a book, it is essential in leading the reader into the page. The best photograph and text are literally useless if they aren't read. Layout assures reading.

Editors and designers ought to study other books and magazines to sharpen their taste and perception. The works of the masters are the best textbooks in any art.

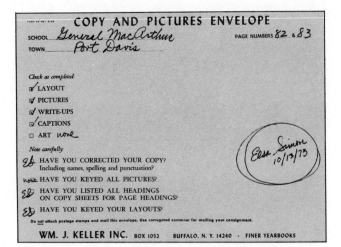

ALL COPY FOR SPREAD is contained in this envelope, which is also checklist for editor. Note that though pages are designed and sent to printer in two-page spreads, facing pages are not necessarily in same signature. Therefore it is always necessary to take care to complete signature as promptly as possible.

On this example, editor who has assembled and checked material in envelope has signed her name (right center) and initialed checklist at left.

Envelopes like this are not designed for mailing and should be placed in corrugated container to protect photos. Details of shipping vary, depending on printer, but basic methods remain same.

"SIGNATURE" is single sheet of paper on which are printed several book pages, always in multiples of four. Placement of pages is called "imposition." Diagram at left shows how eight pages of first signature are printed; back of sheet carries other eight.

Diagram A shows how signature is first folded, halfway on long dimension. In B, second fold has been made in opposite direction, and, C, final fold. Signature is then sewn in fold and to preceding and/or succeeding signatures. In final trimming process, just before cover is attached, folds (as that at top of page 1) are cut open to make conventional book.

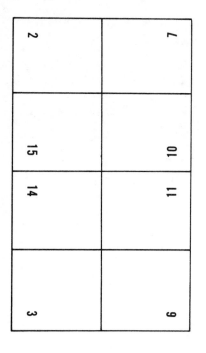

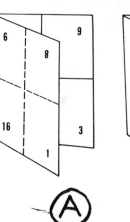

Color

6

... Spice for a Good Meal

Color is a yearbook luxury. If you can't afford it, shed no tears; some of the finest books ever printed were in plain black-and-white. If you can afford color, you must learn to use it properly.

Color can make a good book better; but it cannot make a poor book good. In fact, improper use of color can make a good book poor.

Color must be used functionally or it will add nothing to a yearbook.

Functions of Color

The first function of color is to "augment the image." There are things that color can say better than black-and-white can . . . or that black-and-white can't say at all. A color picture of your school, surrounded by fall foliage, says far more—directly and by evocation—than a black-and-white picture can.

The second function is to help guide the eye through all areas of a layout. Color has strong optical magnetism; so a tiny spot of color will lure the eye despite the competition of larger typographic elements.

The third function is to enhance the pleasure of the reader. Each color has an effect on the reader that is entirely independent of the copy or layout. Red is exciting; blue—the favorite of a majority of people—is calm and cool. Yellow suggests sunshine and all its happy effects; violet suggests the richness of royal robes. Green, brown, and orange are other colors that are enjoyed by most people.

Each proposed use of color in a yearbook must be evaluated, and, unless color performs at least one of the three functions, it should not be used.

It takes great willpower on the part of the editor to eliminate nonfunctional color. There is always temptation to overuse color because, once the initial premium has been paid, it costs no more to use color lavishly than sparingly.

But the key to successful color is using it in small quantities.

A common abuse of color is to run inferior color photographs only because they were available. The editor must insist on superior standards for all photography, black-and-white or color. Blurred focus, overexposure or underexposure, unwanted motion, and poor composition are not hidden by color; usually they are emphasized.

The editor should always choose a superior black-and-white over a mediocre or poor color shot. There is nothing inherently superior in color. Indeed, some pictures are better in black-and-white, since color can be so distracting that it obscures detail and communication.

A layout must always be strong in black-and-white before color is added. If the layout is not basically sound, color will not improve it.

Usually two elements on a spread are all that can be handled effectively in color. If there are more color elements, they will usually compete among themselves for reader attention.

No matter how large a color element is, the total area of color must be markedly smaller than that of black ink. Color must be an accent; if there is as much color as black ink on a spread—actually or apparently—there is no accent.

Process Color

Process color, the most expensive, is the optical sleight-of-hand that reproduces, in printer's ink, the natural colors of the complete spectrum.

Original copy for process, or *full color*, is a color picture. It may be hand art; it is usually a photograph or transparency.

By means of optical filters, the platemaker creates *color separations* of the original copy; he breaks it down into components of the primary colors—red, yellow, and blue. A halftone printing plate is made for each color.

Tiny dots of the three colors cluster in little rosettes that are invisible to the naked eye. When blue and yellow dots snuggle up side by side, the reader's eye doesn't discern individual dots; instead it sees a mass of green. Red and yellow dots give the illusion of orange; red and blue, of violet, and so on. By varying the size of the dots and the combinations of the three primary colors, all the myriad hues, tints, and shades that the eye can distinguish can be reproduced on the printed page.

Color separations are expensive. Original artwork for process color is expensive. The need for three color plates and three trips through the printing press obviously adds to the cost. It is easy to see that many high schools just can't afford it.

(Yet costs of color are coming down constantly. Electronic equipment makes separation faster and thus less costly, and new techniques in photography also help bring process color into the capability of more staffs each year. Before you write off its possibility for your book, you might discuss it with the printer.)

Some yearbook printers make process color available at no cost—usually for end papers. They use color as a premium to reward those staffs who sign contracts early and get certain copy in on an advanced deadline. Full-color end papers add much to a book, and it is well worth the effort of meeting earlier deadlines. The only actual cost to the staff is for the color photo or transparency used.

Spot Color

Spot color, or *flat color,* is much simpler and less expensive than process color. But it can be highly effective.

Spot color is used for printing all kinds of typographic elements; for a background on which black elements are *over-printed;* for adding areas of color to a page or piece of art.

Spot color may be used in any hue. There may be any number of flat colors on a page, although, in yearbooks, only one added color is customary. If more than one flat color is used, it can be combined with other hues on the page to create a new color as well as tints and shades of it.

More frequently, flat color is used for line work instead of halftones. Unless the spot color used for printing halftones is a very deep one, detail will be lost. Brown, navy blue, and maroon are among the

few colors that have enough strength to carry halftones.

Colors for printing type must be equally strong. The same deep colors that must be chosen for printing halftones will usually carry type of any size. Some inks will be strong enough for printing headletters but won't provide enough legibility for body type; most greens, jade blue, orange, and many browns come in this category. Yellow cannot be used for any type, no matter how large; it just can't be read. Red should not be used for body type; it may be heavy enough for readability, but it irritates the eye.

An effective use of spot color is as a *tint block.* This is a large area of color, without any detail, upon which type or halftones are overprinted, or *surprinted.* To make sure that there is enough contrast between black type and the background, the tint block is usually *screened down* by the Ben Day process to lighten it. Yellow and yellowish-orange are the only common colors that can be surprinted without screening.

Screening produces a *tint* of the original color. A *shade* of that color can be produced by printing a fine pattern of dots or lines in black over the full value of the colored ink. Thus the editor has several values of the flat color to work with.

An effective use of spot color is to create a background for a silhouette halftone, which is printed on the white paper, not on the color. Or areas of color may be laid into a line drawing. For these, the artist makes *mechanical separations.*

The artist draws his picture, the *key plate,* as he conventionally would, in black India ink on white drawing board. This is the image that will be printed in black in the yearbook.

Over this he affixes a sheet of clear *acetate,* an *overlay.* Again using black ink, he draws on the

"REGISTER MARKS" on this two-color divider page are familiar cross-and-circle device in top left. Key plate is printed in black; other is printed in—despite misspelling—orange ink.

acetate those lines and masses that are to appear in color in the book. It doesn't matter what the second color may be, the drawing is always done in black ink.

To create a color background for a halftone silhouette, the artist will draw a white outline on the glossy to show where the background is to be removed. On the overlay, he draws—in black—those areas that are to be printed in color.

Duotones

Duotone is a bridge between process and flat color. Original copy is a black-and-white glossy (although black-and-white hand art can also be used).

Two printing plates are made from the single glossy. One is used for a light color, the other for a dark one (usually, but not necessarily, black). The result is the creation of a third, new color. If, for instance, black and yellow are used, the printed reproduction will show neither of these; instead, the whole picture will be in sepia.

The appeal of a duotone is an added—almost three-dimensional—depth to the picture.

Duotones are far less expensive than process color; they cost only a little more than black-and-white. The light color of the duotone is the flat spot color of the page; so the editor can use duotones on all pages of a flat-color signature.

When color is used on any page of a signature, it may be used on all others of that signature at practically no extra cost. Pricing varies and should be discussed with your printer. He can help the editor determine how to make best use—and most economical use—of available color.

Often color is used only for divider pages; duotones are very effective here. Sound planning may enable the use of color on each divider by printing only two or three color signatures. Again, consultation with the printer can save money.

Although they are technically not colors, black and gray are used as such, often as backgrounds, black for white type, gray for black or white type. Often these *achromatic colors* are used as blocks or strips in a layout. Such use rarely creates a pleasant effect; the designer who avoids large areas of black or gray will have far better chances of achieving a strong layout.

When a full-color picture is to run on two pages, it should be placed only at the center spread of a signature. We have already noted the problems of alignment when a black-and-white picture runs across the gutter. In process color printing, these problems are aggravated to such an extent that the editor cannot even hope for satisfactory results when he dummies full-color pictures on pages other than the center spread.

Colored Paper

Color may be added to the yearbook by the use of tinted paper. This is a little more expensive than white paper, but the cost is not excessive. Use of cream-colored or eggshell-colored paper is a custom that dates back many decades. But using other hues is a new technique.

When colored paper is selected, care must be taken to choose a tint that will give adequate contrast to black ink. If flat color is available, choosing the ink and paper in the same color usually results in the happiest effect.

Complementary color combinations should be avoided: blue and orange, yellow and purple, red and green, etc. Red ink on green paper is a particularly distressing combination that pains the eye.

Often a pleasant effect can be obtained by using colored paper for just the opening signature of the book.

End Papers and Covers

Colored end papers usually cost no more than white, and this is often the only opportunity the editor has to get a little color inside his book. He should give special attention to the selection of end papers and to the choice of inks used for printing them.

The cover itself is an effective method of using color. It must harmonize with the color used inside the book, either in paper or in ink.

The cover is assurance that every editor will have some color to work with in planning his yearbook. Inside color is but a bonus for the designer. He must always design the book so it will be strong in black-and-white. Then color should be added only functionally and organically.

Color Photography

If your book is using process color, it adds another factor to the preparation for photography. If your budget can stand it, have a professional take your transparencies. (We assume that *transparencies*,—we commonly call them *slides*—will be your copy. Color photos—be they made by negative-and-printing or as Polaroids—are more costly and usually less satisfactory.)

But whether it's a pro or a student photographer who is doing the job, he should make three exposures of every picture. This does not mean to shoot the same subject three times with minor variations in pose or composition; it means exactly the same photo but with three different exposures.

A light meter should be used for all color work. The first exposure is that one indicated by meter readings. The second exposure should be a little over the meter reading and the third one a little under. All three slides should be sent to the platemaker so that he can choose the one that will

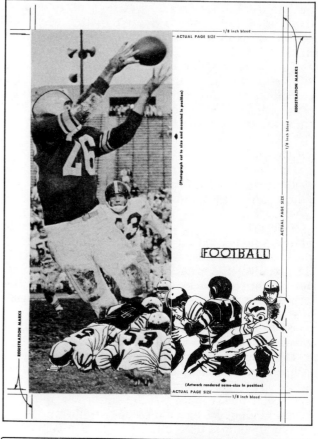

"SPOT COLOR" requires "mechanical separations." First "key plate" is prepared, carrying most detail. (This is usually—but not necessarily—one printed in black.) Photograph and artwork are pasted into proper position and "register marks" drawn in corners. Over key plate, layout man places . . .

. . . "OVERLAY" OF TRANSPARENT PLASTIC or tracing paper. On it artist draws elements that will appear in color. No matter what color will be used in printing process, artist uses only black India ink. Occasionally, if area is large, he may cut out appropriate shape in red acetate and paste it into position. (To camera, red is same as black.)

Note "register marks" in corners here. Register marks of all colors must match precisely during printing process, which then will produce . . .

FOOTBALL

. . . "TWO-COLOR JOB." Element shown here as gray is actually bright blue—cyan—in yearbook; photo, hand art, and type are black. Once register has been made exact on press, marks are eliminated when paper is trimmed, as in this example. If such marks must appear in other areas, they are scraped off printing plate once perfect register has been achieved using scrap paper.

make the best reproduction. Ironically, the transparency that seems best to the naked eye often has imperfections that are not seen until separations and enlargements are made.

(We ought to note here that practically all transparencies must be enlarged and that this procedure works well. A good 35-millimeter slide—⅞ × 1½ inch—can be blown up to 3½ × 5 inches with excellent results. Other standard sizes—2¼ × 2½, 2¼ × 3¼, and the 4 × 5 most often used by professionals—can be enlarged to full-page size, and even larger, as for book covers. Colored photos will usually not withstand such enlargement, and black-and-white photos are normally made large enough so they can be reduced —*shot down*—in platemaking.)

Before expending money on a color picture, ask whether the subject is properly colorful. This author has just seen a picture of a baseball team stretched out along a set of bleachers. The top third of the picture was the pale blue of the sky, unrelieved even by clouds. The lower third was a strip of springtime grass, hardly even green as yet. The "picture" itself was the team wearing conventional gray uniforms, which added no real color. Here was an obvious case in which, black-and-white would have been entirely adequate, and the money expended for color was completely wasted. Of course, the unimportant background and foreground should have been cropped; apparently the editor left it in because he realized it was the only justification—however slight—for using color.

Color shots must be well planned. Backgrounds should be selected with greater care and for their color. Student models should be hand-picked and they must be told beforehand what colors to wear. If the group is small, uncoordinated colors may clash painfully. If the group is large, you may find that the uncoached models all happen to wear the same color that day.

Scheduling color shots is more difficult than for b&w. In most parts of our country, fall and spring are the most colorful seasons. Planning must be far enough in advance to take advantage of the settings that nature provides. Color demands excellent lighting. On outdoor shots you must avoid early morning or late afternoon shooting that distorts color with a reddish or bluish cast. And you must give yourself plenty of leeway so that pictures scheduled for a day that turns out rainy or cloudy can be rescheduled without breaking final deadlines.

Make sure the cameraman knows exactly what the editor has in mind for the layout so that he will pose the subjects to fit the layout area that will be given to the picture.

The best way to examine transparencies is on a *color-corrected* viewer, a slanted, frosted-glass easel with a light behind it. But this is certainly an unnecessary luxury. Good results may be obtained without any equipment. Place a sheet of white paper on a table. Place a light of at least 100 watts about as far behind the paper as your eyes are in front of it. The light should be at least two feet above and two feet behind the paper, and it should be shaded so that it doesn't shine right into your eyes. (A conventional fluorescent desk lamp is a fine light source.) View the transparency with the light reflecting through it from the paper. Never hold a transparency toward direct light; unless it's in a color-corrected viewer, there will be a distortion of colors.

If transparencies must be cropped, there are two ways of doing it. The first is to use the transparency as a film; make an 8×10 b&w photo of it. Steel yourself; this is not going to be a very beautiful photograph, as it will be in negative value that results from using a positive instead of negative film. And the tones will be rather muddy. But it will be sufficient for indicating cropping.

The other way is to lay tracing paper over the transparency and indicate the area you want used. Care must be taken that the pen or pencil used is not pressed into the slide.

The best solution, of course, is to compose the picture with such care that it can be used completely. Alas! This is a little too Utopian, however. But it emphasizes the need for good planning and preparation—on the editor's desk and at the site of the shooting—before the shutter is clicked.

The woman of charm and good taste keeps her cosmetics invisible; garish rouge, lipstick, and eye shadow look cheap and tawdry. Color in a yearbook should be like color on a woman's face.

Never use color just because it is available. Demand even higher standards of it than you do of black-and-white photography. The amount of color used and the amount of money expended on it are no indication of its effectiveness. Use it sparingly, wisely, and in good taste.

Covers
7
... The Box for a Jewel

A diamond ring would be beautiful and rich in a brown paper bag. But because the value and beauty of any object are enhanced by its packaging, rings are placed in handsome, plushlined boxes. The good yearbook also deserves an appropriate package, the cover. We may not be able to "tell a book by its cover," but we are certainly more strongly drawn to one bound in luxurious leather than one with a plain paper cover.

The choice and design of the cover is a major decision of the staff and should be given all the time and attention it requires. Each of the several important factors involved should be considered in detail.

There are three basic requirements for a cover: it must be appropriate; it must be durable; it must fit in the budget. After that, there are so many possible variations that choosing is like going past a smorgasbord line.

Binding Methods

Most yearbooks are bound in the style of the book you are now reading, *sewn-round and back.* It is made up of a group of little sixteen-page books, *signatures,* each of which is *saddle-sewn* by stitching through the fold. Each signature is sewn to the one before and after it until the whole book is a single unit. *End papers* are glued, by a narrow strip of paste, to the book on one side and, by overall adhesive, to the cover. The *spine* of the book has been rounded, and the spine of the cover curved. It is protected by a strip of sturdy fabric. A deep crease where the front and back covers join

the spine serves as a hinge and also helps hold the book in the cover. This makes a durable binding, good almost indefinitely under normal—and even hard—usage, and the pages lie flat when opened.

Inspection of the book you are now reading will illustrate many of these features.

Smaller books, of eighty pages or less, are simply *saddle-sewn* or *saddle stitched,* in a single signature of which the cover becomes a part. Stitching uses staples instead of thread; this binding is used by most magazines.

Because saddle binding is visible on the cover, the effect is not as polished as might be desired, so the small book may be saddle bound and a separate cover glued on, hiding the thread or staples.

Less frequent is the use of *mechanical binding.* Plastic combs are often used. Prepunched sets of pages are placed on the teeth of a comblike strip of plastic, and the "handle" of the comb then curls around to make a half-tube. The plastic comes in a wide variety of color, and—if the diameter of the half-tube is large enough—printing may be done on it by silk-screen. A similar binding, Wire-O, uses a series of connected wire rings. These methods provide no spines, although it is possible to paste on a separate cover to hide the binding.

Cover Styles

Hard covers, such as the one on this book, are the basic style for yearbooks as well as other books. Sturdy *boards,* onto which the cover fabric is pasted, give good and enduring protection to the book.

In *padded covers,* a layer of soft padding is placed between the boards and the cover fabric. The effect is pleasant and rich.

Paper covers—in heavy weight—are used for saddle and mechanical bindings.

Standard sizes for boards and padding for books are 7¾ × 10½; 8½ × 11; and 9 × 12. The covers themselves are slightly larger so that the projection adds to the protection of pages. Any variations on these sizes increase costs markedly. So does binding a book on the short, rather than the long, dimension. Such a format is called a *landscaped* one. Square books also cost more than the conventional shape because they require many adjustments to machinery that has been standardized for the customary specifications.

Cover Materials

Most yearbooks are covered in imitation leather. The plastic material is coated with *Pyroxylin* making it durable and washable.

Pyroxylin is also used to impregnate *buckram* and other *book cloth* to strengthen them. Such covers are almost as washable as those of imitation leather and will not show fingerprints. *Natural cloth,* of which *monk's cloth* and buckram are most widely used, makes handsome binding.

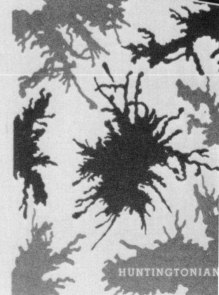

COVER DESIGNS produced by several printing methods. "Chinook" has "wraparound" full-color picture of skyline of Pullman, Washington, where college is located. General hue of photo is blue and spine of book is blue also. Lithography printing produced this.

"Silhouette" is "silk-screened." Cover is light olive, hourglass and letters are black, outer frame is burnt orange.

"La Vieu" has sand cover with brown lettering. It is letter-press.

"Indiana University" has black background, white lettering, and folds of flag in red for attractive and strong design. It is silk-screened.

"Huntingtonian," done by lithography, also has wraparound design in red and blue on white background.

Cover papers are far less prosaic than their name indicates. They come in several weights and a wide range of finishes, many of which look like leather.

Fabric, natural or synthetic, is classified by weight. The best is *3.60 sheeting*, which means that a piece 3.60 yards long and a yard wide weighs one pound before coating. Lighter weights can be used, but the saving in cost is not substantial, and the decrease of wearability is serious.

Cover Printing

The book cover carries the name of the book—sometimes that of the school—the year, and, usually, some decorative element that ties in the theme of the book. There are seveal methods of placing this material on the cover.

The classical cover is *embossed;* the image is raised from the surface of the cover. This method uses two metal *dies,* concave and convex, between which the material is molded. This is basically the same as the hand device used for embossing seals on legal documents or impressing a name and address into personal stationery.

Modeled embossing creates a *bas relief,* a low sculptured image that resembles that on a coin. This is the most expensive method because the making of the dies requires precise handwork by highly skilled craftsmen.

Plane embossing is plain embossing. Large areas are raised like a plateau but only in one plane instead of the several levels of modeled embossing. Often this raised area is the background for an image printed by one of the other methods.

Opposite of embossing is *debossing* in which the image is lower than the surface of the cover. This is done by *stamping,* driving the image into the fabric by a die or type. Sometimes certain lines in modeled embossing are debossed.

These relief methods are technically not printing because they do not use ink. Actual printing methods are *lithography, silk-screen,* and *letterpress.*

Lithography, also called *offset,* places an image on paper or fabric by the same method by which you might draw a picture on a rubber eraser, press the rubber to paper and *set off,* transfer, the image. Lithography can print on rough surfaces and is ideal for a heavily textured cover fabric. Type and pictures can be offset, and a comparatively new technique is to print a photograph—black-and-white or full color—over the entire cover.

(The book you are now reading has a Pyroxylin-treated cover. It is washable, soil-resistant, and damp-proof . . . and guaranteed for the life of the pages. Printing is by offset lithography. The artwork is in line, and two colors are used, black and orange. The white is the color of the cloth.

The method could just as easily have been used for reproducing a photograph in two, three, or four colors.)

In silk-screen, ink or paint is forced through stencils, sometimes cut by hand, but are usually prepared photographically. Silk-screen colors, especially paint, can be brilliant, and this is the only feasible method for printing in white, or a light color, on a dark background. The process can handle type or illustrations. The latter are hand art rather than photos.

Letterpress, or *relief* printing, is the oldest of all methods. Type and illustrations are raised, like the face of a rubber stamp. Letterpress is used almost exclusively for paper covers.

Any printing method may be used on any relatively smooth fabric, and combinations of the five methods are common.

Often an image is printed on the cover by any of the three methods, and then embossing is done. Such products are called *brilliant* embossing or stamping. When no color is used, only the difference in plane defining the image, it is called *blind* embossing or stamping.

Letterpress or offset may be used to produce images with fine detail with silk-screening laying down large, simple masses of more brilliant color.

Any printing method can produce images in one or more colors.

Another pleasing method of adding color is the *overtone* rub. By hand, pigment is rubbed over the entire cover or an embossed area with a soft cloth. Further rubbing with a clean cloth removes the excess color from the high planes of the image and grain and leaves the full color in depressed areas and crevices of the grain. Clear shellac adds luster and protects the color. The most pleasant effect is obtained by using a *tint*—a light value—of the fabric color.

By means of a stencil and an airbrush, a *halo effect* can be placed around a printed or embossed image.

A rather new process is called *metal appliqué.* A sheet of extremely brilliant metal is placed on the fabric. In a single operation, the two materials are embossed and fastened together by a combination of heat and adhesive. The embossing is made more obvious by the shadows cast by the raised image on the bright surface; the metal never dulls by tarnishing. Metal appliqués are especially handsome when used for school seals or simple insignia.

For books on a very tight budget, a colored picture may be *tipped on,* pasted onto, the cover by hand. The results are not as durable as might be desired, although a sheet of clear plastic may be laminated over the front or whole cover to bond the tip-on to the cover.

TRADITIONALLY STYLED COVERS. "Vassarion" has "stamped design," punched into cover fabric. Title and some flowers are in pink; other flowers are blue; background is black.

"Interpress" cover is light blue with "embossed" lettering raised "Overtone" of gold lightly highlights whole cover and lower line of title is in solid gold color.

"WeWaTumpka" is most elaborate. Dark blue cover is "grained" and title is embossed. Circular device is brilliant silver "metal appliqué," which framed "tipped-on" full-color photograph.

"U of M" has "debossed" (pressed-in) grain. Title is metal appliqué of shiny gold, and light steel-gray color is rubbed onto brown cover material.

Cover Designs

Besides identifying the book, the cover design sounds the opening note of the theme. Illustrative material should be bold and simple. The quality of the artwork must be superior. Type, too, must be of the finest quality and this precludes the use of handlettering in all but rare instances.

The cover design includes that on the spine or *backbone,* that part exposed when a book stands on a shelf. Copy is the name and date. Unless the name is short and the book thick, the title cannot be run horizontally without excessive hyphenation that usually creates a poor design and lowers legibility; so the copy must run lengthwise on the spine. The American custom is to run type from top to bottom. The reader must then tilt his head to the right to read the title on a shelf; this is less comfortable than cocking the head to the left. But the top-to-bottom placement means that the title can be read normally when the book lies face-up on a table.

On photographic covers, the design usually *wraps around;* the single picture occupies front and back covers as well as the spine.

Color and texture of cover fabric add much to theme development. There are so many choices available that the staff can easily find the precisely right fabric.

An interesting yearbook used the theme of opening doors. The cover was in fabric that closely simulated wood grain and on it metal appliqué made hinges and keyhole as well as the name. Another staff used the theme of a new building; its cover was blue with white printing and reproduced faithfully one of the blueprints used for the building. A school using an Old West theme naturally chose the grain and color of saddle leather, and the printing was in dark umber; then the images were debossed to give the effect of branding.

Of the many, many kinds of grain, the most popular are *Levant, Morocco, mission,* and *whirlpool.* These are fine grains that do not conflict with any design.

Other grains simulate burlap, linen, and knit wool. All the regular leather grains—pigskin, cowhide, alligator, etc.—are available.

Book cloth comes in several textures. Embossed designs require a fine weave. Silk-screen can be used on even coarse fabric. The surface of cloth, not nearly as smooth as that of plastic, is pleasant to the touch and adds tactile pleasure to visual ones.

There are so many colors available in all materials that it becomes a case of "You name it; we have it."

Artwork for most cover designs is a drawing in black India ink on white paper. Even plane embossing and stamping dies are made from such copy. Instructions for modeled dies may be a sculpture or a drawing to which are appended instructions drawings alone cannot show.

If more than one color is to be used, the staff artist prepares either a color picture or does a separate black-and-white for each color. Many yearbook printers have a staff of fine artists who can do finished artwork from sketches submitted by the staff.

If the cover carries a lithographed picture, copy for a black-and-white is a conventional glossy. On an overlay, the editor indicates where the type matter is to run.

For a full-color photographic cover, the copy is a transparency. This may be made by a professional or a student photographer and ought to be at least 3 × 5 inches.

End Papers

End papers should be considered as part of the cover and chosen and designed at the same time. The papers should harmonize or contrast with the color of the cover. If the cover is dark blue, a lighter tint of blue makes pleasing end papers; a complementary color, yellow or orange, may be used for contrast. With light covers, a darker end paper is effective. Using the same color and value for the outside and inside of the cover is usually less attractive.

Any color paper and/or ink may be used for end papers. The paper itself can—and usually is—textured in one of the several styles readily available. Naturally, the paper must be sturdy; it is the only connection between book and cover.

The more ornate the cover, the simpler the end papers should be. A stark cover allows a more detailed end paper. A popular trend is using a long-range exterior shot of the school. Another is to create an overall pattern of the same device, often the school seal or emblem. The printer can create such a design by the *step-and-repeat* method, which requires the staff to furnish only one copy of the element. A pleasing effect is to screen down all the repeated elements except one. That one, in full value, gains emphasis and affords interesting contrast.

It is customary—and most economical—to use the same design for both front and back end papers. But the cost of two designs is not excessive, and sometimes the subject matter can best be handled by using two. You might, for example, use the front and back view of your school . . . if the latter is pleasant and doesn't show garbage cans and housekeeping paraphernalia.

Often the two designs are identical except that the one at the front has a built-in *bookplate,* with the customary copy: THIS BOOK BELONGS TO . . . or the classical EX LIBRIS (*from the books of* . . .) and space for the owner to write his name.

Absolutely plain end papers are attractive (and

cost the least) and are fine for autographs.

A new opportunity is offered by at least one printer. He furnishes stock end papers that show—in full color—pictures of outstanding news events of the year from the whole world. Such a collection of individual pictures, gathered into a single unit, is a *collage*. It is a difficult technique to master. Surely it is one that a student staff can rarely perform with good results. These stock papers are inexpensive and, in many instances, are the only way in which the staff can afford full-color photography.

Use of stock end papers means that it is difficult, if not impossible, to use them to develop the theme. But this is not a fatal disability by any means.

Standard Covers

Many staffs have to work on a tight budget. This should be accepted—not as a cruel blow of harsh fate—but as a challenge. They can reduce the cost of covers by using *stock designs* or reusing existing dies.

Most covers are manufactured by a separate firm, not the printer. Sometimes the covers are shipped to the printer, who affixes them to the book. More frequently, the sewn and shaped book, or even just flat printed sheets, are sent to the cover manufacturer, who does the entire binding job.

These manufacturers have thousands of *stock dies*, designs with wide applications: warriors, of mythological or knighthood era; Indians; floral designs; and, for religious schools, a variety of crosses and symbols. Abstract, geometric designs are countless.

The largest cover manufacturer in the country offers some thirty textures, over half a hundred colors, at least that many overtone tints, and a huge inventory of design and title dies. They add up to well over 50,000 possible variations.

This large number reduces to negligible the danger that your yearbook will have the same cover as that of a neighboring school. If, by the weirdest of coincidences, this should happen, the manufacturer—if he is doing both covers—will notify the staffs in time for them to make changes. Stock dies of different manufacturers will be different, of course, and so exact duplication of covers by two companies is impossible.

Many schools reuse the same die, year after year. The school seal—which is an increasingly popular motif—is particularly effective as a recurring ornamentation. Its reuse eliminates the cost of new dies, which may run from $65 to $100 for simple plain ones to as much as $300—or even higher—for those with elaborate modeling.

Reusing a motif need not create monotony. Its position on the page, the color of fabric and ink and overtone, if any, and the use of metal appli-

qué can make each year's cover fresh and appealing. Meanwhile, the continuation of a motif gives a pleasing relationship among all the books and is a tradition worthy of respect.

Cover Trends

Staffers should be wary about trends. Too often a trend is merely "a bright idea followed by a horde of imitators." On the other hand, a trend may help a staff define its needs and its solutions.

"The trends of the 70's," according to Frank J. Mohring of Wm. J. Keller Inc., a major yearbook producer in Buffalo, "include covers in bright colors, especially hot pinks, reds, and lemon yellows. Photographic covers have grown greatly in popularity, partially because of the upsurge of photography on the campus and also the special effects that are possible (through photomechanics)."

Padded and embossed covers are dropping rapidly in poularity, he says.

Most observers agree that the trend in design is toward utmost simplicity, and school seals are used with ever-greater frequency.

CONTEMPORARY COVER is lithographed in black on white background. Because shape of book is so traditional and unmistakable, even most unconventional cover design may be used without losing recognition.

Smaller schools can often squeeze two-color photography out of their cover budget if four-color is unfeasible.

Pyroxylin-coated materials are most popular; embossing is used on the greatest percentage of yearbooks. Linen or natural finish are most always chosen when book cloth is used. Stamping or silk-screen is always used with cloth covers. Lithographing is done on Pyroxylin-impregnated cloth or plastic.

The trend to light covers has introduced the use of clear plastic *slip jackets*. These are sturdy covers made with pockets into which the book covers are slipped. Jackets are usually custom-made so that they fit smoothly, and the plastic is so clear it has no effect on the appearance of the cover. They are sold as an "optional extra," just as in the automobile trade; no student is required to buy one along with the book.

Slip jackets are practical. They protect the book and can easily be washed when they accumulate too many fingerprints. But to many observers—including this author—they tend to cheapen the effect. His personal preference is toward a cover color that is dark enough to withstand the most obvious of casual soiling. And, unless the cover is of natural cloth, it can be cleaned with a damp cloth and mild complexion soap.

Cover Budgets

Saddle stitching is the least expensive binding method, but can be used only for small, one-signature books. Saddle-sewing is only a little more expensive, but it, too, is practical only for books of eighty to one hundred pages.

Mechanical bindings are comparatively inexpensive. Some staffs even do the actual binding themselves; equipment is low-cost, and the process requires little skill.

Sewn-round and back is the most costly.

Paper covers are the least expensive; then come conventional hard covers, and, most expensive, padded ones.

Letterpress and lithography are the least costly printing methods. Letterpress is used usually only on paper covers. In increasing cost are stamping, plane embossing, and modeled embossing.

For images in more than one color, silk-screen is least costly—if the design is kept simple. For pure color, overtone is most economical. Reproduction of full-color photographs is by offset and is most costly.

There are so many variables in covers that the only definitive answer on cost is reached by discussion with the representative of the printer or cover manufacturer. Indeed, the staff should never make decisions on the cover without professional advice. And this advice should be followed.

Covers usually cost from 15 to 20 percent of the total of producing a book. Too frequently, a staff will skimp on the book proper to provide an expensive cover. This is foolish. The content is still more important than its package. To choose a design that requires excessive cost is to admit to a lack of true creativity. To choose a cover of inferior quality will mean that the book will become dilapidated long before its normal lifetime. It is better to have a good book with a cover that represents real creativity, than a mediocre book with a cover that indicates only the expenditure of money rather than thought.

The suggestion of that last sentence applies to all aspects of yearbooking, of course. A great book is created; it is not simply purchased from a printer. And it is far, far more fun to expend enthusiasm, creativity, ingenuity, and plain old hard work than to spend even a lavish amount of money.

If there is a single, final, and all-inclusive word of advice to a yearbook staff, it is: "Have fun!"

It is no coincidence that the copy that has been the most fun to write, the photograph that has been the most fun to set up and process, the spread that has been the most fun to lay out . . . that all these give the greatest fun to the reader, too.

That must always be the aim of the editor and his staff: to make a book that will best serve the reader. In making your yearbook the reader's book, you most truly make it your book, too. It will be your scholastic monument, one that you will be proud of for just as long as your book is read, reminisced over, and enjoyed by even a single one of your classmates.